Be Encouraged

God Is With You

BARBARA SAXON

Title: Be Encouraged, God Is With You
Author: Barbara Saxon

Publisher & Editor:
Shakima's Publishing Company LLC

Illustrator:
Barbara Saxon

ISBN: 979-8-234-03820-3

Printed in the United States of America.

Scripture quotations are taken from the King James Version (KJV) of the Holy Bible unless otherwise noted.

This book is a work of spiritual expression and personal testimony.

Foreword

This collection of poems was written through seasons of prayer, reflection, and lived experience. Each poem is a reminder that God's presence is constant, even in moments when life feels uncertain, heavy, or overwhelming.

These words were not written from perfection, but from perseverance. They are offered to encourage the weary, strengthen the faithful, and remind every reader that God is near, attentive, and actively working in their lives.

May these poems serve as a source of comfort, hope, and renewed faith as you walk your own journey with Him.

My Heart On Paper

To My Daughter, Anicia Rachael Saxon Turner ("Nicee") November 6, 1979 – June 5, 2022

To my firstborn, who carried her name with the grace of the Holy Spirit: you were "God's Best" a nurturing soul who saw me through every season of life. As your middle name, Rachael, suggests, you were the embodiment of gentleness and devoted love.

You were the one by my side when I first heard God's call, and you were the one who documented my journey when I couldn't find the words myself. Thank you for loving me through the good, the bad, and the ugly, and for leaving behind a legacy of brilliance in your son, Stephen. You fought the hard fight against Sickle Cell for 22 years, and while I miss you every day, my heart is at peace knowing you are no longer suffering. You were, and always will be, my heaven-sent angel.

My Testimony of Grace: Isaiah and Gabriel

I also wish to recognize my sons, Isaiah and Gabriel. You are more than just my children; you are my living miracles. When man and science said "never," the Great Physician said "now."

My Heart On Paper

When I was in the fast lane at the peak of my addiction, headed toward a mental institution, prison, or an early grave, God's mercy said NO. He knew how to put the brakes on. He saw a woman He could trust to stop using and bring two precious souls into this world healthy and whole. You are the reason I chose life, and I am eternally grateful that the Lord trusted me with you. You have grown into two powerful men of God, and I love you beyond measure.

"To be absent from the body is to be present with the Lord." 2 Corinthians 5:8

Acknowledgements

First and foremost, my heart overflows with gratitude to Almighty God, who chose me before the foundations of the earth were even laid. (Ephesians 1:4) I am a living testament to His grace. He has saved, healed, delivered, and set me free. He is not a distant memory, but a living, breathing presence in my life. I am humbled to be led by the Holy Spirit and deeply blessed to hear His voice.

It is the greatest honor of my life to pen these words and messages sent directly from His throne to breathe hope into the hearts of the lost. I give Him all the glory, standing as proof that what He has done for me, He is ready, willing, and waiting to do for you.

To Bishop Edward Black, thank you for those gentle, spirit-led nudges that kept me moving toward the finish line. Your belief in me gave me the strength to finally see these books into print.

To Pastor Glendon Jones, a man of Godly character and much wisdom. Thank you for the prophetic word that prompted me to write this book. I thank God for you and your obedience.

Acknowledgements

To Tina Sims Taylor, my dear friend of fifty years. Thank you for the countless hours and the vast energy you sacrificed to help me reach this moment.Your support and patience have been my anchor. If I ever seemed ungrateful in the heat of the work, please know that my heart was always full of appreciation. I love you more than words can say.

To Ms. Wooten, my 9th-grade English teacher: you spoke a prophetic word over my life before I even understood what that meant. You saw the "Great Writer" in me when I was just a student learning to write limericks to release my feelings. Thank you for recognizing my gift and encouraging me to never stop.

To Bianca Thomas, thank you for being such a profound blessing to this journey. My prayer is that God pours out a lifetime of favor and open blessings over you and your entire family.

To Shakima Walker, my publisher: thank you for accepting the assignment of bringing this vision to life with such grace. Your dedication has been a vital part of this journey.

Acknowledgements

It is my prayer that as you hold these pages, you feel the heart of the Father. This work is His gift to the world, shared through me.

Be Encouraged: God Is With You

"Have I not commanded thee? Be strong and of a good courage; be not afraid, neither be thou dismayed: for the Lord thy God is with thee whithersoever thou goest." Joshua 1:9 (KJV)

TABLE OF CONTENTS

Volume I: Foundations of Faith

——————————————— Be Encouraged, God Is With You

TABLE OF CONTENTS
Volume II: Walking In Christ

Be Encouraged, God Is With You

TABLE OF CONTENTS

Volume III: Victories In His Presence

—————————————— Be Encouraged, God Is With You

TABLE OF CONTENTS
Volume III: Victories In His Presence

Be Encouraged, God Is With You

TABLE OF CONTENTS

Volume III: Victories In His Presence

———————————— Be Encouraged, God Is With You

Introduction

Be Encouraged, God Is With You is more than a collection of poems. It is a testimony of God's unfailing love, mercy, and faithfulness. Each poem reflects moments of struggle, surrender, healing, and victory, offering encouragement to those facing life's trials.

Through personal experience and spiritual insight, these poems speak to the heart of anyone who has ever felt broken, lost, or unsure of their purpose. They serve as gentle reminders that God sees, God knows, and God remains present through every season of life.

As you read, allow these words to minister to your heart. Take what you need, reflect deeply, and be encouraged in knowing that you are never alone, God is with you.

His Perfect Will

ROMANS 12:1-2

His Perfect Will

I thank God for not allowing the devil to afflict my body with AIDS. I thank God for not allowing me to O.D. or to be killed. I'm not proud of my life but I'm happy to tell my story for the Glory of God to save someone's life; to save souls for God's purpose. I use to be lonely and bored and I thank my God for choosing me and filling my life with His Holy Spirit and Power to do His Perfect Will I don't have time to pity myself. Nor, do I have a reason to pity myself.

Romans 12:1-2 (KJV)

"I beseech you therefore, brethren, by the mercies of God, that ye present your bodies a living sacrifice, holy, acceptable unto God, which is your reasonable service. And be not conformed to this world: but be ye transformed by the renewing of your mind, that ye may prove what is that good, and acceptable, and perfect, will of God."

United Unto God

EPHESIANS 4:21-23

United Unto God

United Unto God
The Spirit of the Lord doesn't flow in a click, to only certain races, places and members. That would cause a blockage, poor circulation and malnutrition. Are you blocking your blessing or killing yourself? Where the Spirit of the Lord is there is life.

Ephesians 4:21-23 (KJV)

"God says, love everyone, greet every saint and especially the people of the world. And the Grace of God will be with you. If you can't lift up or encourage your brother and sister in the Lord, how can you be a good witness for the Lord? He that wins souls is wise. If a tree doesn't bear fruit, it will be cut down."

DATE   /   /

♥

Open Up The Door

Open Up The Door

Who's there? This may be your chance at entertaining an angel unaware.
She may be a whore shacking next door. It may be the thief caught stealing seek after week. It could be the drunk stumbling up and down the block.

You've just blessed your home and you're resting and relaxing in your comfort zone.
There's a knock at your door. Will you welcome this soul and receive a blessing or be arrogant, vain and pride filled and lost forever more?

The Lord sends souls so that His gospel can be told. If there's a knock at your door and you're in the right plan with God welcome them in although they're in sin. Let them in and let God's work begin.

So, have no fear. For in the Word it is said, one person in the Name of Jesus living right and being prayerful can put one thousand demons to flight and two ten thousand. So, open the door and be a witness for the Lord.

♥

Children

PSALMS 127:3-5

Children

Children are precious
Children are jewels
Children are gift's that God lends to you
Children are a blessing; tender and sweet
Children are not for you to mistreat.

Children are innocent, they learn what they see - so be careful to keep your life honest and discreet Children are good they have hearts of gold. Be careful your actions lead to their future and the mind that you mold.

Psalm 127:3-5 (NIV)

"Children are a heritage from the Lord, offspring a reward from him. Like arrows in the hands of a warrior are children born om one's youth, Blessed is the man whose quiver is full of them. They will not be put to shame when they contend with their opponents in court."

DATE / /

Kingdom

Kingdom

In the Kingdom
there is no room for baggage
No room for boxes
Just a whole lot of praising
There will be no tripping
No falling, no back biting
Just praising all the day long
Get ready - Praise Me!
Jump, stomp, shout, clap!
Get your dance on!
For the Lord is surely coming back
So, praise Him
Praise Him again and again
This is how it's going to be
So, shout
Hallelujah and Amen!

Business

Business

B e about Gods Business
U live Holy
S anctify yourself
I keep your eyes on Jesus
N ever underestimate God
E asy is His yoke is
S tand
S tay standing no matter what

BUSY NESS

Make sure your business is God's busy ness or it will bring you to sin. It will B. U. - SIN so, it is Ness... Necessary for you to live Holy and Sanctified. Separate from sin.

The Diet

The Diet

To Good Physical, Spiritual and Mental Health Dedication and Determination...Reaching towards the Prize of a Higher Calling. Acknowledging God with praise and worship. Not over indulging in anything. Putting no-thing before Him.

Involving yourself in physical activities as well as spiritual. Outreach, walking for Christ with prayer and fasting. Always keeping the flesh under subjection. Exercising your faith daily. Believing, and eating properly from the Bread of Life.

Total resistance of the enemy. Turning away from, knowing that you are free.

He whom the Son sets free is free in deed. Go for your goals knowing all things are possible in Christ.

Into His Kingdom

Into His Kingdom

You cannot make it into
the Kingdom of Heaven
without the name of Jesus.
Jesus told Peter, except ye
be baptized in the name of Jesus.
Jesus said that you cannot
enter into the Kingdom
Except you come through Me.
Your prayers do not
reach the Father except
through the Son.
Your sins are forgiven
when you ask in the
name of Jesus
You cannot enter with the
name of Jehovah,
Buddha, Muhammad, Allah

DATE   /   /

♥

Please Excuse My Smoke

Please Excuse My Smoke

There is no excuse to smoke. We smoke because we want to - no excuse. It's our choice to live clean and Holy. It's our choice to live polluted in sin - no excuse.

The warnings are written on every box or carton; smoking may cause cancer. We think it's pleasure. It is also written in the Word of God, where there is sin come death. So, no excuse if you smoke.

Live in heaven eternally with peace, praise and tranquility. Or die in hell with pain everlasting. Being tortured by the demons of the past and smelling the stink and stench of burning flesh. So, no excuse. It's your choice.

If you choose to smoke, you choose death.
If you choose Jesus your life will be blessed. Let the Blood of Redemption excuse the past. Please excuse my smoke.

notes

DATE   /   /

♥

Keep Your Eyes On Christ

Keep Your Eyes On Christ
Don't Be Distracted

Keep your eyes on Christ for He is our guide. Keep your eyes on Christ. If you should look away you could stumble and fall. Keep your eyes on Christ for He is the way, the truth and the life.

Keep your eyes on Christ for straight is His way and narrow is the path to the Gate. Should you look away, you will veer to the left or the right. Keep your eyes on Christ. He is your balance. If you should fall look up to Him unto the hills for where cometh your help. Keep your eyes on Christ He is your life. Take away the distractions and look for the coming attraction.

He is coming back!

Granny

Granny

The time has come we all hate to see when our loved one leaves us here to go home to be with our Father; The Almighty King.

Times with Granny were full of joy and laughter. She was a woman who kept love in her heart. The kind of love only God can give.

Granny endured a lot of pain. Trying hard not to complain. She was full of courage and strength. Granny will never have to suffer again. For she has returned to her Maker's Hands.

No matter how Granny felt, she was always very nice; never giving unwelcomed advice.

When you're feeling lonely and want to cry lift your head to the sky and know that Granny's pouring out blessings from on High.

Granny finished her course and showed us the way. So, follow the instructions given and you will see her face again inside the Pearly Gates.

Let Go & Let God

PROVERBS 3:5

VOLUME 1: FOUNDATIONS OF FAITH

Let Go & Let God

It's time to let go and let God.
For He is the Master of all things.
He is the Teacher of all teachers. For He is the Giver
of Knowledge and Wisdom.
He is the Doctor of all doctors. For He is a Healer and
Creator.
That which He made, if it should get out of order,
He will put in line and order.
He is all knowing. He knows the number of every
hair on our head. He sees all and knows all.
He is God Omnipotent, Omni Present, Always there.
Don't be set in your ways. For our ways are not
God's ways. And His way is the only way.
He is the Way, He is the truth, He is the light of life.
So let go and let God.
For Without God, we are nothing - no thing
Let go and let God.
Through Christ I can do all things.
For He is the God who gives me strength.
A very present help in the time of trouble
Let go and let God
He can do anything but fail
He is Perfect in all ways. ***Proverbs 3:5***

♥

The Infinite Mind Wants To Know

The Infinite Mind Wants To Know

I care about you and I hear you when you pray. But there is something that you did not say. I want to know about your day. Do you have a problem? Or do you have a Praise? I want to know about your life and all about your stress and strife. I see you struggle and I can feel it when you press.

Yes. I already know all and see all that goes on in your mind and in your life. I want to hear it from you. Open your mouth and begin to confess. All I want to do is bless and give you beloved eternal rest.
In your business, I will not poke or pry but I have all the answers to your what's and whys. I want to know because I am your only help.
Not like your so-called friends. (man) You can't always depend.

Someone said, "Inquiring minds want to know." Why do they want to know? So, they can share with someone about you and throw your personal business straight to hell.

The Infinite Mind Wants to Know

Well, my friend tells me.
Avoid all the grief and pain. I Am the Infinite Mind with
no limit. I can do all things but fail. In Me you can
always lean and depend. I am Jesus. The one Who
knows your end. I Am the One with the winning plan;
with unchanging Hands. I don't play both ends against
the middle for I Am the Beginning and the End.

The Infinite Mind wants to know in which direction you
want to do. If needed.

I Am able to deliver you from all sin before your end is
Hell. I care. I want to wipe away all tears and bring joy
and prosperity in the time you live and dwell.

Catch The Vision

PROVERBS 29:18 KJV

Catch The Vision

Do you see My Face?
Here I stand with open arms
Can't you see My Face?
I'm calling My People to a Higher Place.

Do You see My Face?
Here I stand.
Humble yourself before Me and Pray
Pray, Pray, and Pray

Do you see My Face?
Can you see My Face?
If not, you've been blinded
By sin and disgrace. Turn away and repent
Now, before it's too late.

Can you see My Face?
Just look up!
Look up towards the hills where cometh your help.
There you will find Me your Lord and strength.
Do you see My Face?
Can't you see?
I am the giver of Grace and I am the giver of Peace.

Catch The Vision

DO YOU SEE MY FACE?

Can't you see?
I Am
The Giver of Grace and Peace?
Do you see My Face?
Can you see?
Catch the vision
Rejoice!
Give me praise
Get ready
I want to take you to a
Higher Place!!
Without the Vision
People perish

Proverbs 29:18 (KJV)

*"Where there is no vision, the people perish:
But he that keeps the law."*

You Are My Bride

You Are My Bride

You are My Bride.
You are married to Christ.
All other men may reject you.
They may not like you and disrespect you.

I will protect you.
I will keep you.
I am your Husband and you are My Wife.

I do Love, Honor, and Cherish you.
In you I take Pride because you are My Bride.

There is NO TOUCH that can do you like mine.
I Satisfy, Heal, and Meet every need.
Live Holy!

Give me the Glory for you are My Bride.
I gave up My Life.

Remember Redemptions Story

notes

God Cannot Be Put In A Box

God Cannot Be Put In A Box

64

God cannot be held in a box or put in a box if He lives in you and you live in Him.

How can you allow yourself to be put in a box?
There is no limit to God.
So, how can you be limited with Jesus in your life and your eyes kept on Him?
You can reach and Goal.
So, go all the with God.

In Jesus Christ the Solid Rock I stand. All other ground is sinking sand.

notes

DATE   /   /

No, No, I Won't Go

No, No I Won't Go

Sin called and said "Come go with me". I said "No, No, I won't go I love Jesus".

He has delivered me and made me whole. He saved me from my sin sick soul. He's healing me the hurt is gone. So, to sin I say "No, No I Won't Go." Jesus comforts me when I'm feeling low.

He's even there when I feel alone. He gave His Word in Him I can trust. So, get Back Satan, I won't go.

Jesus gave me life and life brand new. Jesus freed me from bondage and the grip of death.

He left me with the decision the light of Life or Darkness and Death.

I choose life and I say to sin "No, No, I won't go."

Well Done

Well Done

Cooked at a temperature that flesh cannot bear. Brought for rid of all impurities. Not in the raw. Not naked, well-seasoned easy tender hearted. No longer tough easy to work with. A willing heart.

Meat gained through trials and tribulations wounded. Heated with fire, nurtured and seasoned nourishing to the body. Making strong giving life, strength, good health and energy. A process of being made whole (Holy). Dead to the world yet very useful.

God's people are the salt of the earth being brought through the fire of every trial and tribulation. By His Grace and Mercy for His Glory we will be used to lead the lost to Him. So that He may begin a Good Work and Finish being brought through the fire being changed into pure gold So that we may hear Him say Well Done thy Good and Faithful Servant.

Well Done!

♥

Down But Not Out

Down But Not Out

You may be down in the valley low in Spirit. You may feel depressed, burdened and sad. You may be oppressed and bound. In the name of Jesus be free, You may be down level to the ground.

Heart broken in sin. Hearts Jesus can mend and he also is a forgiver of sin. But, just know Jesus is your way in when you're out of the ark of safety. Just know as long as you live there is hope.

You can live and not die. Jesus is the way. You may be down in a mess. But Jesus is waiting. He wants to bless you, give Him a chance. Surrender all and raise your hands. It may seem you're lost, in the wilderness of confusion, deceived to believe that the only way out is death.

But Satan is a liar. Jesus is the way, the truth and the life.

Down But Not Out

Glory be to God, for another day of life. He is the light, the way out of darkness. You have been chosen to live and not die. Glory be to God the giver of life. By His grace you've been down but, not out.

Come to me all that are burdened and heavy laden, and I will give you rest. For my yoke is easy and my burden is light.

Relationship Put Together By God

MATTHEW 19:6

Relationship Put Together By God

I'm in love with a man; he truly doesn't understand
The love that I have for him is according to God's
purpose and plan.

I'm in love with this man, and I have no reservations.

It is a love that came with no hesitation.
It is a love that requires no explanation.
I'm in love with a man, and this love is not a
coincidence but a
testament to God's ordination and orchestration.

This love is larger than your imagination.

My faith in His plan is unwavering, and it is this faith
that fuels my love for this man.
I'm in love with a man who has known me since the
beginning
of time and God's creation.

I'm in love with a man and don't care who cannot
comprehend.

Relationship Put Together By God

This is love, and this man is all a part of God's master plan.

What God has put together, no one and nothing can tear apart.

It is a love that transcends time and space, a love that is eternal. *Matthew 19.6*

Are You Walking Or Just Talking?

Are You Walking Or Just Talking?

We all can talk the Jesus talk,
but, can we all walk the Jesus walk?
We were all sent to serve Jesus Christ and do
whatever He wills in your life.
Remember, Jesus gave up His very life so that we may
walk in His light.

A light that shines through our actions and services.
Do you truly understand the divine plan?
For it is said "walk by faith not by sight" and "without
faith it is impossible to please God" so truly believe
because only then can you receive.

For a man says,
"Seeing is believing," but with man, seeing is
deceiving. Some believe what they hear, but it is in
God's Word,

Are You Walking or Just Talking?

"Eyes have not seen nor ears heard.
Jesus Himself says,
"Trust and obey, for there's no other way.
" So, close your eyes
to man's lies, keep your eyes on the prize, and follow
in the divine light.
Let the Holy Spirit be your guide. Hold onto the
Words of Jesus, for He has the keys.Only then will you
be pleased.
Don't just speak the words, praise the Lord to me.
Give Jesus the capital Praise Hallelujah for that's the
highest and most.

Blood and Water: H2O

REVELATION 1:5

Blood and Water: H2O

People often say, "Blood is thicker than water,
" and yes, blood is thicker.
This phrase means that blood kinship is
more important than that of our friends or a stranger.
We do not realize that the blood and water of a
stranger, Jesus, saved our lives. Without the stranger
(H2O), there would be no relationship.

Water is just as powerful as blood, for without water,
the blood would not flow properly due to its
thickness. People also use the phrase,
"Weak as water," but water is not weak.
Water is found in every living thing.

Water brings life; water causes oxygen. The chemistry
is Hemoglobin 2 Oxygen.
If it weren't for other people in the world, a man would
meet a woman he never knew; they would be
strangers.

After the two are united in marriage and
consummation occurs by intercourse,
the connection of flesh and blood takes place.
A new life is formed.

Blood and Water: H2O

Remember, it takes two. When that life comes forth, first the water, then the blood, then the new life, the two become a family with a new life.

When the soldier pierced Jesus in the side with his sword, he was trying to bring confirmation to the death of Jesus. Instead, he brought forth life. When the water flowed out of Jesus' side and mixed with the blood, it brought forth power in the blood.

Water is a cleansing agent; without the flow of water, the blood is at a standstill, stagnant. Like soap, it cleans and kills germs, but without water, it just covers the dirt, while flowing water washes it away.

Water also helps prompt healing; that's why plasma is found in the blood and is a potent healing tool. Jesus' blood covers sin, brings new life, does many things, even heals. It is mighty. The baptism with water, H2O, washes away sin.

When you pray with a repented heart, asking for forgiveness, Jesus' blood covers sin, and the tears of repentance wash away, showing sincere sorrow for the sin committed.

Blood and Water: H2O

Water is just as important and powerful as blood. The two need each other to flow and operate correctly. We all need each other.

Be careful not to discount anyone; love and care for them as you do your own, for we all are related by the H2O of Jesus Christ. The stranger that shed His blood on calvary and the power of His resurrection.

There is power in all of us and through each of us, and our testimonies to the glory of God is healing for someone else. So be blessed and receive the H2O. Young or old, rich or poor, we all have the same God, and in our veins flows from His to our H2O: hemoglobin 2 Oxygen, the blood and water of Jesus Christ.

Revelations 1:5

"And from Jesus Christ, who is the faithful witness, and the first begotten of the dead, and the prince of the kings of the earth. Unto him that loved us, and washed us from our sins in his own blood."

Blood and Water: H2O

Matthew 3:16

"And Jesus, when he was baptized, went up straightway out of the water: and, lo, the heavens were opened unto him, and he saw the Spirit of God descending like a dove, and lighting upon him."

John 4:14

"But whosoever drinketh of the water that I shall give Him shall never thirst; but the water that I shall give Him shall be in Him a well of water springing up into everlasting life."

DATE   /   /

Check Yourself Before You Wreck Yourself

PSALMS 133

Check Yourself Before You Wreck Yourself

We are the body of Christ, and God lives in us and through us. We should flow together smoothly in love, with all members of the body communicating in unity.
Psalm 133

All members of the body should walk and work in the Spirit, not in the flesh, because in the flesh dwells no good thing.
Ephesians 4:12-16

We as saints should be bearing fruits that are true, noble, just, pure, lovely, of good report, bringing virtue and praise.
Philippians 4:8-9

These fruits of the Spirit should be seen, felt, and heard of you. The life of a saint should bring light where it is dark and everywhere they go.
God doesn't have any favorites. He is not a respecter of person.
Acts 10:34-35

His blood was not shed for a select few; it was shed for all so that we may live and not die.

Check Yourself Before You Wreck Yourself

The Spirit of the Lord doesn't flow in a clique to only certain races, places, and members.

A clique would cause a blockage, poor circulation, and malnutrition. Are you blocking your blessing or killing yourself? Where the Spirit of the Lord is, there is life. God says love everyone, greet every saint and especially the people of the world, and the grace of God will be with you.
Philippians 4:21-23

If you can't lift up, or encourage your brothers and sisters in the Lord, how can you be a good witness for the Lord? He that wins souls is wise.
Proverbs 11:30

If a tree doesn't have fruit, it will be cut down.
Matthew 7:19

notes

DATE   /   /

God Is Pure And True

God Is Pure And True

God doesn't want us to take the quick
and easy way, for there are no shortcuts to Jesus.
He can only make something instantly good or
instantly healed, not man. Jesus doesn't need
additives or preservatives.

He is fresh, pure, and true.
He can preserve all things all by Himself. Jesus is
faithful and sincere. Nothing is fake or false with Jesus.
Nothing is hidden with Jesus, for He sent his Word.

I thank God that I no longer need substances to
comfort my pain, for Jesus sent his comforter, and
there is no substitution for Jesus.

He is everything pure, true, and just. He is love. There
is no greater love than the love of Jesus,
and no man can have it unless he has Jesus.

Nothing about Jesus is hidden by lies, for He is truth,
and his truth doesn't need to be covered or coded,
for he is good and God Almighty by himself.

Satan is a liar and deceiver, and He uses men (flesh)
to carry out his lies through manipulation. For the devil
is a wolf in sheep's clothing.

God Is Pure And True

All things of the devil appear to be beautiful, fun, and good until he grabs hold of you. Then, it is utter destruction, pain, and misery.

The word devil is even coated for the word is evil with a "D" in front for the D stands for death, for he is the death angel. His job is to steal, kill, and destroy.

Everything about God is good, for he is love, and there is no evil or "D" for darkness or death in him, for He is Life and Light. God is good even to the end. Every day with Jesus is sweeter than the day before.

To God be the glory, the creator of miracles!!!

God Won't Let You Fall

God Won't Let You Fall

Do you feel lost?
Could it be because you think you're the boss?
Do you think you're in charge of your life?
Do you think you're grown and on your own?

Well, never can it be for Jesus paid the
price for you and me.
Only in His will can you learn and be totally free.
Free from sin, and only then can you win
and have the victory.

Jesus is the boss, for He paid the
unmeasurable cost.
He was sent by the Father
and charged to sacrifice His life,
for only He could pay the ultimate price.

If you think you're grown and your life is your own,
that's where you are wrong.
For Jesus bought us with His life,
the ultimate price.

He died a terrible and undeserving death,
yet He stayed on the cross so that we
wouldn't be lost.

God Won't Let You Fall

Jesus took another step after His undeserving
yet purposeful death.

He went down into hell, He bruised Satan's head,
and He rose with the keys,
having power over all things.

If you feel lost, remember who is the boss
and not one battle has He lost.

If you trust and obey Jesus, He won't let you fall.
To God be the glory, the creator of miracles!

DATE / /

Growing Pains

Growing Pains

I know I'm existing, yet no longer is it me.
The Spirit of God lives and dwells in me and is
constantly cleanses me. My heart is aching, and it
even feels like it's breaking, but I know it is God
making and molding the new me.

I'm crying out to you, Lord, because my flesh can't
stand the pain, and Satan keeps flashing memories
of my past in my mind again and again.

Lord Jesus, please help me see your guiding light.
My desire is to be perfect in your sight.
I've looked left and right, and all I see is death,
destruction, and the end of my new life.

Jesus, won't you send forth your comforter and help
me make it through one more night? I know that you
are here because I hear your voice telling me to stand,
not faint, and keep my eyes on the prize. Don't give
up because I've already won the fight.

Jesus, please help me; I've used every spiritual tool
and kept every golden rule. Yet this pain is killing me
inside, and all I do is cry; please deliver me into the
wonderful fruits of Christ and take away the torment I
feel inside.

Growing Pains

I know trials and tribulations come to pass.
In the end, I will be blessed only if I continue to hold your holy hands of righteousness; and allow you to kill my filthy flesh.

Jesus, please help me endure the pain. I know that you and only you are my strength, and I have been saved by your wonderful and amazing grace. That is enough for me.

-To God be the glory, the creator of miracles!

How Do I Love Thee?

2 CORINTHIANS 12:9-11

How Do I Love Thee?

The love of Jesus
I love thee more than thine own self,
I love thee with all my spirit and with strengths
indescribable.

I love thee more than any man or woman ever can imagine.
I love thee when you're weak,
I love thee when you're strong.
When you are weak, say you are strong, for I am your
strength. *2 Corinthians 12:9-11*

I love thee when you are right and
even when you are wrong.
Understand?

I love thee with a love unconditional, but, no one can
I love thee, and you don't know why.
You think that you're no good and not worth my time. My
time is my time, not man's.

I created you in my image,
and I've seen all I made as good.
Genesis 1:27, Genesis 1:3

I am God, and I am love. I am also your judge.
No man is perfect, and in no man's heart dwells any good
thing. *Romans 7:18*

With love everlasting and eternal.
Your Father

notes

DATE   /   /

♥

I Am Who God Says I Am

I Am Who God Says I Am

I am a crybaby, and He collects all my tears.
I am His child, not a brat.
I shout, I stomp, I kick, I give praise.
I am His seed; He created me in His image.
I am His, no matter what.
I am the best I can be;
only Jesus knows the plans He has for me.
I am blessed by the best and He has favor over me.
I am His and He is mine until the end of time
because Jesus loves me.
I am saved and I continue to praise
because in Him I believe.
With Jesus on my side and Him as my guide,
I can pass any test and have victory.
With Jesus, I can do all things;
I am a miracle in progress.
I am that I am.
I am who Jesus says I am.

Jesus Is The Key

JOHN 14:6

Jesus Is The Key

You cannot enter the Kingdom of Heaven
without the name of Jesus.
Jesus told Peter, except ye be baptized in the name
of Jesus. *Acts 2:38*

Jesus said you cannot enter the Kingdom except
come through Me. Your prayers do not reach the
Father except through the Son. *John 14:6*

Your sins are forgiven when you ask
in the name of Jesus.
You cannot enter with the name of Jehovah, Buddha,
Mohammad, or Allah or any other name.
Except the name of Jesus.

Jesus is the door; ask in My name,
and it shall be done.
Knock in the name of Jesus,
and the door shall be opened.

No other name under Heaven
or on earth can save us.
Except we be born again of the water
in Jesus name and the Spirit.

Jesus is the way, the truth, and the life. *John 14:6*

notes

DATE / /

Just Like A Flower

Just Like A Flower

Roses are red, white, yellow, pink, and even black.
Violets are blue.
God created flowers,
just like He created me and you.

Flowers grow toward the light of the sun,
and sometimes need food and water.
Remember, just like a flower,
Jesus created me and you.

Jesus is the light of life;
His word is our spiritual food.
His Holy Spirit gives us living water.
For without it, like a flower,
we would wilt and die too.

Jesus, the son of God, holds all power.
Even over the April showers,
because He creates the May flowers.

His love showers and rains on us,
and gives us spiritual and physical strength to see
each day through.
If you lack one ingredient from above
like a violet, you seem blue,

Just Like A Flower

Or, like a dead rose, your petals are black,
and people seem to turn their back.
Remember, like the sun shines on a
flower to dry the morning dew.

Look to Jesus; He will give you peace and new life.
As the sun shines on a flower to dry the morning dew,
Look to Jesus. He will dry your tears for you!

-To God Be the glory, the creator of miracles!

Keep It Moving

MATTHEW 5:39

Keep It Moving

Stop the violence

God's Word says resist not evil or he that is wicked.
Matthew 5:39
No, that doesn't mean go looking for it
or purposely placing myself in harm's way.
Turn the other cheek.
If a man smacks you, keep it moving.

If a person steals from you, give them more.
Luke 6:29
It's all about God.
He doesn't want us to be pushovers
or punching bags,
but He said the weapons of our warfare are not carnal
but mighty through God. *2 Corinthians 10:4*

So put down the guns and knives.
Jesus laid down His life so that we may have life
and life more abundantly. *John 10:10*

Stop the violence

He rose in 3 days with all power and victory.
The battle is already won;
we don't have to fight each other.

Keep It Moving

Know that we in Christ Jesus are redeemed from the hand of the enemy. *Psalm 107:2*

Kept safely wherever we go. *Psalm 91:11*

Getting all of our needs met by Jesus. *Philippians 4:19*

So cast all your cares on Jesus.
Know that He will protect you, Provide for you,
He will never leave you nor forsake you.
Be not moved by what you see,
Walk by faith and not by sight, *2 Corinthians 5:7*

Keep it moving.

Don't you worry.
Don't you fret.
Walking with Jesus, you won't regret it.

Is it a peace that you need?
God will give you peace that surpasses all understanding.

Is it joy that you want?
In Christ Jesus, there is joy unspeakable.

Keep It Moving

Is it rest?
Are you tired and don't feel like you have
the strength to go on?

Well, God says in His Word, "Come unto me,
all ye that labor and are heavy laden, and I will give
you rest." *Matthew 11:28-30*

Seek God while He may be found and keep it moving!

notes

DATE   /   /

♥

Know Jesus Lives

Know Jesus Lives

Jesus said to know He shall never die
and He shall always live.

Do not just think He lives; KNOW He lives,
for it is a fact.
I know.

DATE / /

♥

Never Too Late To Change

ISAIAH 1:18

Never Too Late To Change

If you are weary, He will give you rest.
If you are tormented, He will give you peace.
If you are lonely, He will give you comfort.
He is everything you need.
It's never too late to change.

If your heart is broken in two, He can heal you.
Your life may be falling apart, remember that you're
His work of art.

He will make you whole.
It's never too late for change.

Your sins may be as scarlet;
ask for forgiveness in His name.
Isaiah 1:18

God is just to forgive your sins. Never to remember
them again.

He will throw them as far apart as the east is from the
west into the sea of forgetfulness.
Micah 8:17, Psalm 103:12

Never Too Late To Change

He will change them white as snow, to be remembered by Him no more. *Isaiah 43:25*

Come to Jesus and be saved, let the old man pass away. Become a new creation, start today. *2 Corinthians 5:17*

It's never too late to change!

Reach For My Hand I'm Your Friend

MATTHEW 6:33

Reach For My Hand I'm Your Friend

Hello, my friend, I'm right here to give you a hand. You've tried everything else known to man, and it has failed you again and again.

I've come to let you know that you don't have to go any further, for you are being used to commit your own murder. I'm knocking, won't you let Me in, for I am your only hope.

I've come to let you know that you don't have to go down that dark and dreary road, for I've been here and there before. I was saved by Grace and filled with the power of the Holy Ghost.

I have all the joy you won't find in drugs, so why won't you give me a chance to share my love? I am the creator of heaven and earth, and I even knew you before your birth.

Sin seems to have you bound, and you can't seem to stand. Remember, you have a friend, and I'm here to give you a hand.

You will never win the battles of this life unless you let me in. I have the divine master plan not known by any man.

Reach For My Hand I'm Your Friend

I will never enter by force, for the choice is yours, but I am watching the score. You know that you are losing in the Satan's ahead, and if you reject me and continue in sin, your end is death.

Once again, I've come to you to give you a hand, won't you let me in? It's never too late until you lose your breath; you can defeat the angel of death. Just call my name Jesus Christ, for I AM waiting to give you a new life.

Don't worry; just relax. I'm a true friend, willing to forgive you of every sin and able to rid you of your past. I am the way, the truth, and the life, and always your friend.

I am here to let you know that you don't have to go or look back down Death's Road. There is no need to place blame or even be ashamed; make higher ground your aim.

You don't have to die in distraction and the evil ways of men, for I can deliver you from all sin and change your state of mind. I am God you're only true friend, I will never leave or for sake you that you can always trust in, lean on and depend.

Reach For My Hand I'm Your Friend

So won't you open the door? I'm knocking, just grab hold of my unchanging hand. Hold my hand tight, keep me in your sight, and follow me in the light, for there is no darkness in me.

Your ever-loving, everlasting, eternal life giving friend. I know your every need and want. I say to you, "Seek ye first the kingdom of heaven and all of its righteousness, and all other things shall be added unto thee." *Matthew 6:33*

There is hope for tomorrow. Won't you let me take away your sorrow?

To God be the glory, the creator of miracles!!

The Great I Am

The Great I Am

1. I am Jesus, the one who laid down His life on Calvary for your sins and rose again with all power over death, hell and the grave.
2. I am your protector, for no weapon formed against you shall prosper.
3. I am the Alpha and the Omega, the beginning and the end. I was here before the foundations of the earth. I will be here when the world ends.
4. I am your comforter when you're sad and lonely.
5. I am your Father when you're fatherless.
6. I am love when you feel unloved.
7. I am your provider when you're in need.
8. I am a peacemaker when your enemies come in like a flood.
9. I am your creator, I created you from the clay of the earth.
10. I am God, omnipotent God, all knowing. I know every hair on your head, I know your thoughts, what you're going to say or do before you do it.
11. I am God, all mighty. There is now power greater than I and beside me is no other. I and my Father are one

The Great I Am

If anybody asks you who I am, I am the great I am, the way, the only way thru Heaven's gates.
I am the truth for I cannot lie.

I am the giver of life and the taker, for your life is not your own. I am the one who laid down my life for sin's ransom so that you may have life and life more abundantly.

I am a comforter to those that are burdened and heavy laden. I bid you, come unto me and I will give you rest.

I am a Father to the fatherless. Abba, Father, I say unto you, be ye baptized in the name of Jesus and receive my spirit being born again. For without me, you are fatherless, a bastard, and a man without God is a heathen – wild and lost.

If anybody ask you who I am, I am the great I am.
I am above and never beneath; I am the winner of all wars. I am the one who began a good work in you and I know your end. I am the great I am.

notes

DATE   /   /

The Love of God

The Love of God

All the things God has done for me,
His favor, grace, and tender mercies.

I look back on my sin and how deep I was in it.
He could have let me die a miserable death; that is the
wage of sin.

But no, He reached out His hand and invited me into
His master plan, the light, out of death, despair, and
darkness.

The love of God we may never comprehend,
He never sleeps nor slumbers,
He holds all power in His hands.

The love of God is for His purpose and His plan.
God, unchanging and unlike man, shows His Love
through compassion, understanding, and forgiveness.

This is a love we can always depend on.

God's love is unconditional without restraint. God, our
Father, cared so much that He sent His son to hang,
bleed and die to rise again, paying for our sins that we
could live a life of abundance.

The Love of God

God's love is free and it runs deep. His blood runs through our veins with power overflowing that we can overcome anything.

God's love gives us power to sustain our abundant life.

God's love is everlasting and forevermore.

Why Wait To Celebrate

Why Wait To Celebrate

This is the day the Lord has made; let us rejoice. God created Heaven and Earth, and He saw that everything was good. We were created in His image, the best. God is great and greatly to be praised.

Why wait to celebrate?

Jesus died and rose again so that we could live without sin. Repent and be baptized in Jesus' name. You will receive the precious gift of the Holy Ghost. The devil is under our feet; he has been defeated. The victory is ours through Jesus Christ, who set us free.

Why wait to celebrate?

Jesus is my rock, my sword, and my shield; if He be for me, who shall be against me? No weapon formed against me shall prosper. There is no other name in Heaven or Earth where we can be saved. In the name of Jesus, we have the victory.

Why wait to celebrate?

Come on, let's give Him praise!

notes
DATE   /   /

Without Spot Or Wrinkle

EPHESIANS 5:27

Without Spot Or Wrinkle

God is coming back for a church without spots or wrinkles.

Often, we fall into sin and become spotted and dirty with sin.

Our path is not straight; we have weaved a wrinkled web.

Yet, we are not without hope.

For God, who possesses all power in the name of Jesus, has the ability to cleanse us of every spot of sin and straighten out every wrinkle of doubt and confusion.

Be ready and repent.

You and I are the church.

Be raptured without spots or wrinkles. *Ephesians 5:27*

notes

DATE / /

You Are Never Alone

MATTHEW 28:20

You Are Never Alone

You are never alone. There is someone who hears every moan and groan.

You are never alone . There is someone who hears every sigh, even when you cry.

You are never alone there is someone who knows what's hiding inside through tears and fears.

He will give you peace, Jehovah Shalom you are never alone.

There is a man we call God, Jesus, Jehovah Nissi. He will fight your battles.

He has many names; just remember you are never alone.

He's there when you cry.
He feels your pain inside.
He knows your thoughts and what's on your mind.

You are never alone.

You are a perfect work of art.
He knows your heart.

You Are Never Alone

You are never alone; we are His creation.

Even when you've given in temptations, remember you can be forgiven.

Don't let Satan's guilt and depression delay your succession or progression.

Let prayer be your intercession; no matter where you are, remember you are never alone.

Behold, I am always with you until the end of the age.
Matthew 28:20

notes

DATE   /   /

♥

You Don't Have To Die

You Don't Have To Die

I gave my life on Calvary,
All I ask is that you serve me.

I died on the cross and rose again,
So that you could live a life free from sin,
All I ask is that you repent and be born again.

Go down in the water, baptized, washing away sin,
and burying the old man,
Coming up letting your creator in.

I'm not asking a hard thing, to live for me.
I'm not asking you to die; just live a holy life unto me.

I did the dying that you might not perish but live life
and life abundantly. So, stop being selfish and try
living for me.

Be an example.

I want to save your children and your family.
Yes, sin seems fun; the devil's pulling your strings.

I'm letting him play his little game,
But his time is almost up just the same.

The choice is yours.

You Don't Have To Die

I offer eternal life, but if you play with sin, you can be
sure, a horrible death it will be.
But, I paid the price on Calvary,
Just repent and reach for me.

The road is narrow, and the path is straight.
Keep your eyes on Jesus, and He will lead the way.
Set your treasures in heaven,
For this earth is going to pass away.
Jesus is calling. Will you choose life today?

All I ask is that you live holy,
I love you and want you to be free.
I'm not asking you to die, for I did that on Calvary.
I died that you may live life abundantly, a life of
prosperity.

You never have to be alone, and you never have to be
afraid, for I will never let harm come your way.

If you invite me in, I will bring strength.
Heal your body and all your brokenness.

The darts of your enemies will have no effect.
I want your body to be my temple,
Where we can sup and communicate.

You Don't Have To Die

I want you to pray without ceasing, day after day,
Tell me everything, and I will never turn you away.
I love you, my child; I care what you have to say.
Pray in the Holy Ghost, for the Spirit knows what to
say.

I will bring strength and keep you day after day.
If you have a need, let me know when you pray, for I
am your provider; just keep the faith.
Every day won't be easy, for the enemy will come
your way,

But you don't have to die, just kneel and pray.
All I ask that you live holy, trust in my Word, and obey.

You don't have to die.

-To God be the glory, the creator of miracles!!

notes

DATE   /   /

My Hero is Jesus Christ

My Hero is Jesus Christ

Jesus is my hero because...

He died so that I could be saved and have a chance at..

Eternal life. He was...

Resurrected with all power over death, hell and the grave so that I could have power to

Overcome any obstacle that life should pass my way

notes

DATE / /

♥

Good Credit

Good Credit

God
Omnipotent
Omnipresent
Divine

Chosen
Restored
Exhalted
Delivered
I am
Testament

Saved

Saved

Sanctified

Annointed

Victorious

Eternal

Destiny

DATE   /   /

Fake it Till You Make It

Fake it Till You Make It

Faithful
Active
Keeping
Eyes on God

In spite of
Trials

Understanding
Never Give Up
Talking to God
Insist on
Learning the Word daily/Live Holy one day at a time

Y
O
U

Mature in Christ
Accept
Kindness
Equally give

I
Tithe

DATE   /   /

Fornication

Fornication

Faithful
Active
Keeping
Eyes on God

In spite of
Trials

Understanding
Never Give Up
Talking to God
Insist on
Learning the Word daily/Live Holy one day at a time

Y
O
U

Mature in Christ
Accept
Kindness
Equally give

I
Tithe

LSD

LSD

L ife

S aving

D evice

You Are
To Me

You Are To Me

Like the sunshine in the sky, you light up my life.
Like the brightness of the stars in the sky, you put the
sparkle in my eyes.
Like the moon follows you on a dark night from the sky, my
thoughts are of you every day of my life.
Like the wind blows through the trees, your scent brings a
refreshing touch to me.
Like beautiful flowers blossom in on a spring day, my love
for you is more beautiful than a priceless bouquet.

notes

DATE   /   /

Fervent Love

Fervent Love

I love you more than words can say.
I love you in the most infinite way.
When you walk into a room, my mood becomes and lighted, and I'm able to take on the day and whatever comes my way.
When you walk away, I think of how blessed I am to be obliged with the privilege of loving one of heaven's most exquisite jewels.

♥

Forget About Self & Look To Jesus

Forget About Self & Look To Jesus

Just yesterday I had to realize that I was acting, talking and being just like a spoiled selfish brat when I had to realize where I was at. Satan had his paws on m e causing pain and all I could see or think was me, me, me.

Well it took a moment till I fell to m y knees and I said Lord won't you help me please. I took a look at where you brought me from and I said Lord won't you forgive me please.

Today I say Thank you Jesus for you died for me and only in you will I be pleased. There were a lot of things I never would or could have believed that I could do or stop doing. Today through Jesus Christ and the strength and power He has given unto me all things can be done. Again today I can truly say Jesus is all the world to me through Jesus Christ He gives me the victory.

Jesus is my life, my joy, my all for without I would fall.
I often have something toż remind me that can't nobody do me like Jesus He's my friend and in the name of Jesus I have the victory. Oh how I love Jesus for He first loved me and He didn't bring me this far to leave me.

Forget About Self & Look To Jesus

I know I can tell my Heavenly Father, friend, lover, husband, my overcomer, my everything about any and everything and He is always there with a listening ear and He doesn't condemn. He will still love me for me and all that I am. For I am His child and He gave His life for me so that I could have the victory over man and sin.

In Jesus will I trust in Him will I obey and through Gods grace and mercy will I hold to His unchanging hand everyday.

God be the glory, the creator of miracles!!!

I Love You

I Love You

I love you through the joy
I love you through the pain
I love you through the sunshine
And even in the rain
I love you when you are near
And when you are far
I love you when we are together
And when we are apart
I love you more than the day we met
Every day that we spend together
I realized I am blessed

DATE   /   /

True Love

JOHN 14:15 KJV

True Love

True love to me as always, putting God first as Jesus says.
Jesus says, if you love me, keep my Commandments.
John 14:15 KJV
Praise me.
Put no other gods before me.
Exodus 20:3 KJV
Trust me.
Obey me.
Believe in me
Honor me.
Speak boldly my gospel.
Keep your hand in my hand.
Keep holy communion.
Stand still and know that I am God.

True love should be the same with your companion!,
Remember remembering God is the head, without him,
nothing works. Second, the husband is the head over the
house with God as his head. The wife is next under the
husband and God, then the children.

true love and holy matrimony.
first of all, love your companion as yourself.

True Love

Love.
Honor.
Cherish.
Be honest.
Trust.
Believe in.
Respect.
Let no one or nothing come between.
Pray together and stay together.
Stand beside.
Swallow foolish pride.
Keep a listening ear.
Never sleep in anger.
Keep the lines of communication open.
Submit to one's needs.

Being ready to leave, mother and father and taking responsibility for a family, living as one together, enjoying all of God's gifts as one prospering.
Letting nothing and no one steal our love, peace, joy, happiness, and contentment.
For it has been ordained by God and holy matrimony.
The rest of my life I will spend given God the glory and praise.

True Love

Thanking him for a second chance at;
Life, love and romance.
True love is not just for romance, but for the purpose
of continuing God's plan.
And I will keep myself unto you forsaken all other
others!
Bone of my bone, flesh of my flesh.
I love you!

To God be all the glory, the creator of miracles!!!

DATE   /   /

What R U Afraid Of?

What R U Afraid Of?

People ask, are you afraid to be alone?

I say no, thinking I can take care of myself. Wondering if I'm
ready to give up, surrender the relationship
I put my whole existence into, giving him my whole heart
and love him with every ounce of my being.

Time, effort and money meant nothing for me to love,
honor and cherish. Am I scared to be free, or is it the pain of
tangled heart strings? Am I afraid to be alone, or is it
entering back into the twilight zone?

Will I wait for a full recovery, or will I lay in duress. For I have
no heart, I gave my all away. I had such a big heart and it
caused me so much pain. There's such a big hole to fill
before it will beat again.

Will I medicate, will I pray, will I seek treatment; physical
therapy, rehab, or the arms of another man?

That's it, the pain, here it goes again.

Am I losing my patience or am I losing my faith in the man;
the relationship that I put all my hope in.
I'm down for my man, even though he's leaving.

What R U Afraid Of?

I'm shaking my head in disbelief.
How could all my love, all my time and caring, how could it fail?

Oh Lord, feel my pain. All I know is to give to love, to do my best and represent the best, love. Oh Lord, help me through this pain. Lord I acknowledge you. Your will be done. Order my steps.

I'm down for my man, what am I afraid of?
I don't want to give up the faith that I have in you. I don't want to give up on love and relationship. I don't want to do this again. I don't want to make my move too soon. I don't want to lose the man that once made me feel again.
I don't want to let go. Lord, I love him.

Why does it have to hurt so?
Don't I deserve to be happy, don't I deserve to have love, be loved, feel loved, on earth as it is in Heaven?

What happened to everlasting, unconditional, agape love?
I'm down for my man.

Thank you Lord, for never leaving nor forsaking me.

My Love For You

My Love For You

My love for you is greater than the imagination
My love for you helps me defeat every temptation
My love for you are stronger than the vaults at Fort Knox
My love for you is stable and secure and every thought I
have a view is pure and true
So on this day, I renewed my vowels of love to you
Promising to always honor, protect and stay true
I freely give my oath in marriage and propose my love for
you

notes

DATE   /   /

Love & Be Loved

Love & Be Loved

All I ever wanted was...
To love you and be loved by you.
I gave you me,
My all my time, my support,
My heart, my body,
My commitment to faithfulness and loyalty.
I'm your biggest fan.
With a sober and sound mind,
I put my hand in your hand
As part of God's plan.
My love for you was an is incandescent.
When we made love, the climax was effervescent.
Every time I feel our hearts connect,
There stood rejection.
A jerk away, a pushback from a man that my eyes
could still recognize,
But my heart did not know.
My love for you was transparent for you and all the
world to see.
I was so proud to call you, my man.
My love for you transcends from God,
It was His plan.

DATE   /   /

Sin

ISAIAH 65:5

Sin

When does God say about sin?

Sin to God is like riffraff- no good, lowlife, trash- stinks has been discarded, no longer useful. A stench in the nostrils of God.
(Isaiah 65:5)

A child of God live and saved is full of the spirit of God and is not comfortable doing anything or going anywhere.

On the other hand, trash lies where it will or wherever the wind blows. The destiny of trash is in a landfill waiting to be buried never having a chance of being used again by God or by man.

Once the land is filled, the trash is burnt in an open pit of fire, going back to ashes and dust. Blowing around with no peace just a tormented soul.
Destination: hell, the wages of sin is death
(Romans 6:23)

notes

DATE / /

Life Is Like A Puzzle

Life Is Like A Puzzle

Life is like a puzzle
With a million pieces
Sometimes,
Poured out,
Scattered all over the place,
But God knows what pieces fit perfect.

notes

DATE   / /

♥

Shop With Jesus In Mind

THERES NO WAITING OR LINES

PSALM 34:8

Shop With Jesus In Mind

When you shop, remember to not worry about what you shall eat what you shall drink or what you shall wear. For whatever is needed, he will prepare. Jesus is constantly extending an invitation to us that doesn't cost us, like a free sample. "taste and see that I am good." *(Psalm 34:8) NIV*
if you're hungry, Jesus is the bread of life *(John 6:35)*
are you thirsty? Jesus is the fountain of living water. *(John 43:19)*

are you in need of a hairdresser? Jesus knows the number of every year on your head. *(Matthew 10:30 & Luke 12:7)*
whatever it is that you need, Jesus will bear. Just ask in prayer.

Jesus says, praise me, not pay me. Try me, not buy me. Come as you are, not dressed to impress because nothing impressed him more than a sincere heart willing to give him their all heart mind and soul.

Jesus is like wash and wear, for he does the cleaning from the inside out, and he has the power to wash away all your sins; steam cleaned, pressed, sin stains removed, you will be made hole without spot or wrinkle.

Shop With Jesus In Mind

Jesus is a saving consultant. Put your trust in his fund and he will do the saving. He won't steal you blind.

He will open up your eyes and save your soul. Jesus died, paid all your debts and freed you from the devil's grip.

 he will continue to provide all you'll ever need and give you eternal life with the final victory. If you're in need of a blessing, continue to hold to his unchanging hand and your blessing is coming that you can depend.

DATE   /   /

♥

Remember Me When You Look At Your Tree

Remember Me When You Look At Your Tree

The tree represents the tree of life.
The branches are the body and every part of Christ.
The lights represent the light of a life with Christ.
The thistles represent the thorns He wore for a crown.
The star represents the star that shined over the
manger where and when Jesus was born.

The bright, colorful, and shiny ornaments represent
the jewels that are found just lying around on the
Heavenly grounds and even some are in my crown
that awaits me.

The garland represents the bond that should never be
severed or cut between me and Thee.
The green represents the color of life which is the
nature of my creator, Christ.

The red represents the blood that He shed for us.
The white represents pure light and the robe He has
awaiting me. So remember Jesus as you look at your
tree, and remember Christ in Christmas.

Show love and be a happy family, do all these things
in remembrance of me, your Heavenly Father, Jesus
Christ!
To God be the glory, the creator of miracles!!

DATE   /   /

Unto Us A Child Is Born

PHILIPPIANS 4:13

Unto Us A Child Is Born

It is our job to raise them as we raise them.
Lift them up because like us, children fall and when they do, on the precious name of Jesus you should call.
They don't come with instructions, use God's word for directions.

Teach them to trust and obey for there is no other way.
Children sometimes cause us stress, just remember that you are blessed.

Sometimes you'll want to pull out your hair; instead go to God in prayer.
There will be days when you laugh and days when you cry, it gets easier by and by.

Children are lots of fun & always keep you on the run.
Raising a child is a daily walk with Jesus by your side using His Word as your guide.

Children sometimes get in our way because they like to play. They need extra love and attention.
A child will take you to your wits end sometimes to get attention.

Just hold to Jesus' hand.

Unto Us A Child Is Born

Train a child in the way that they should go, before
you know it they will be grown.
When they leave you will they be secure and stable?
Or lost and incapable? *(Philippians 4:13)*

Let your child know, you can do all things through
Christ Jesus who strengthens.
Putting God first in all things, honoring thy mother and
father that their days should be long on this earth.
(Exodus 20:12 & Ephesians 6:3)

Children are fragile and deserve tender loving care,
you can either break them or mold them.
The Word says behold unto you a child is born.
It is up to you to show them the way.

When you're stressed, do your best remembering you
are blessed.
Like any other test, put your best foot forward and
Jesus will do the rest.

Amen!

He Will Take Control

He Will Take Control

It is our job to raise them as we raise them.
Lift them up because like us, children fall and when
they do, on the precious name of Jesus you should
call.
They don't come with instructions, use God's word for
directions.

Teach them to trust and obey for there is no other
way.
Children sometimes cause us stress, just remember
that you are blessed.

Sometimes you'll want to pull out your hair; instead go
to God in prayer.
There will be days when you laugh and days when you
cry, it gets easier by and by.

Children are lots of fun & always keep you on the run.
Raising a child is a daily walk with Jesus by your side
using His Word as your guide.

Children sometimes get in our way because they like
to play. They need extra love and attention.
A child will take you to your wits end sometimes to
get attention.

Just hold to Jesus' hand.

notes
DATE   /   /

Blessings Of God

ROMANS 13:8

Blessings Of God

Remember God doesn't give handouts.
He gives a hand up.
He doesn't give loans, because loans bring debt.
God's will is that we owe no one but to love them
(Romans 13:8 & Proverbs 22:7)
God's blessing is that we be lenders and not
borrowers ***(Deuteronomy 15:6)***
The price has already been paid.
God doesn't give credit,
Because all of the glory belongs to Him.
God makes ways out of no way,
Because He is the way
(John 14:6)
God gives blessings overly and abundantly,
more than we can ask for, think or even imagine
(Ephesians 3:20)
He meets our needs
(2 Corinthians 9:8–10 & Philippians 4:19)

DATE   /   /

♥

It's Time To Rise Up

JOHN 10:10

It's Time To Rise Up

People of God it is time to rise up.
Walk right, talk right, praise God, and let His light
shine
out into the world.

It is not His will that we lay on our back
or on our belly and down on our knees begging,
pleading, lying, cheating, and stealing.

It is His will that we spend time in His presence
and give Him praise and to go out and share His ways
in our testimonies of what He has done for us.

It is His will that we live life abundantly.
(John 10:10)
It is His will that we prosper and have good health.
(3 John 1:2)
So rise up and be about God's business before it's
too late. You don't have time to struggle.
Give it to God and let it go.

Many of you say that "the struggle is real",
Well God is real and He has power to deliver you from
all things. Nothing is too hard for God.
(Jeremiah 32:17)

notes

DATE   /   /

Know Your Assignment

MATTHEW 7:13-14

Know Your Assignment

As you go throughout your day,
remember to pray, see God, seek to hear his voice.
We all have an assignment.

It's no longer business as usual,
As you can see the arrows in the street.
They're just like the path of life going in every
direction.
I pray that you choose the straight and narrow path,
For the road leads to death, hell and destruction.
(Matthew 7:13–14)

No, I'm not perfect and I never have been,
But I have decided to be about my father's business,
And this is my assignment to spread His word.

Don't take sides take over!

DATE   /   /

Why Do Men Cheat?

GENESIS 1:26-28

Why Do Men Cheat?

Why do men cheat when God gave them everything,
even the first woman He gave Adam and Adam named
her Eve.
God had a companion that He gave everything: land,
trees, a harvest, even a world full of animals that were
tamed as can be.

All Adam had to do was name them, relax and feast
and at the cool of the night, meet God.
One evening, God met Adam and said
"You need some rest" and He put him to sleep.

While Adam slept, God performed surgery. He took a
rib. And from that rib, He formed a beautiful woman
that Adam named Eve.

God said that man should not be alone and He woke
Adam up then presented him with an awesome gift
that Adam named Eve.

God, Adam and his friend, his new companion, his
perfect fit, a soul mate, his wife, that God given
woman that Adam named Eve went for a stroll through
the beautiful land of Eden, which was all handed to
Adam to maintain, enjoy and love.

God gave Adam dominion over every living creature.
(Genesis 1:26-28)

Why Do Men Cheat?

Do not eat from one tree, do not touch, do not even think about it. That tree was the one of knowledge. Seek to know no more. Adam, now being the head of now his woman, the animals and the land, had everything handed to him from God. He had only one command, be a man, pay attention, show affection, enjoy the scenery, look but don't touch, enjoy the ride, enjoy the feast.

I gave you, you from your side, your rib, your best, my best woman.

For some reason, Eve was strolling alone and along came a slithering snake, so sly, so slick, full of lots of crap, talking lots of trash. Not much time went by, where was Adam, didn't he miss Eve?

What happened to his connection to God or to his woman that he named Eve?

Why do men cheat?

Were the animals more interesting? Did they need Adam? No, but his woman did. By her side he should have been. Right beside his woman, Eve. His left side, his rib, his heart, Eve. His woman, his helper, help mate, a virtuous woman, the mother of all, Eve.

Why Do Men Cheat?

Why do men cheat?

in my mind, and thought, in action, they drift away, always logging for something else. Why do men cheat?

I don't know why men cheat, and my name is not evil, no matter what my name, I am woman. God's beautiful creation, and I can only be me.

If my name were Eve and God gave me Adam, I would be by his side like a Siamese twin. There would be no time wondering were drifting away to temptation by the serpent.

We would be busy enjoying life, love and each other in God's giving tranquility.

Why do men cheat?

From the moment Eve became bored and drifted away in search of more, feeling neglected by Adam's lack of attention and affection, their connection faltered. Consequently, we are left to grapple with pain, illness, stress, conflict, corruption, hard labor, abuse, and destruction.

Why do men cheat?

Why Do Men Cheat?

God gave man his best everything and a woman. I'm the best I know and beside every good man is a woman, his rib.

Why do men cheat?

Not like Adam and Eve, we don't have it easy. There is so much chaos because of the flesh, wanting to seek more of the tree with the forbidden fruit.

Wanting to know God's plan before it is to be revealed, thinking God is keeping something from you. Wanting to know more like the beautiful angel that got allowed to leave the choir he made beautiful music. He was the most adorned, but he wanted more. He wanted to be God.

Why do men cheat?

The reason for this betrayal lies within that angel, who was cast down from his heavenly orchestra to endure a hellish existence on earth, a realm filled with persecution, torment, and sin.

Why do men cheat?

Why Do Men Cheat?

The angel lost his talent, orchestra and beauty and kept a very small percent of his entourage that fell with him.

Why do men cheat?

As a child of God, I recognize that I haven't always been virtuous; however, my worth exceeds that of all the gold. With God's love, I give my all to Adam. Like God, I experience pain, yet Jesus continues to bless me with strength and grace.

I give, give, give, forgive, forgive and forgive. With love, love, love, trying to stay connected yet I don't understand.

Why do men cheat?

No, I'm not Eve, but I am my man's woman. I've been sent to him by God, faithful, loving, loyal, not even in a perfect world willing to listen and communicate not trying to wonder. Asking, not seeking to know more.

Why do men cheat?

Why Do Men Cheat?

God gave Adam a woman for himself to have, to hold, to love, honor, respect, cherish, to walk with side by side, hand in hand. Everything that man needed with animals and beautiful land that must not have been enough because Adam lost interest.

And then came along a serpent there was just waiting for the moment to whisper, sweet nuts to his woman's ear. She was alone too long and listen then came sin.

No more peace, no sanity, just blood sweat, tears, hard work and labor.

Why do men cheat?

What is this distraction? What is this attraction when you have such a precious gift custom-made to fit your needs and desires?

Why do men cheat?

Walking With Christ

Walking With Christ

We are overcomers by the Word of God.
We have victory through Christ.
Don't you worry!
Don't you fret!
Walking with Jesus,
You won't regret.
It is peace.
It is joy.
It is rest.

DATE / /

♥

Hallelujah

Hallelujah (Lyrics)

Hallelujah l-a-lu-ah, I love you Lord today.
So, now, I praise You.
I thank You for all your love and grace.
Thanks for forgiveness and deliverance today.
Thanks for your blessings, peace of mind, and
showing me your way.
You are omnipotent, omnipresent every hour of the
day.
You are Alpha and Omega, forever and always.
So that's why I praise you, I lift you up, I magnify your
name,
I just wanna say it in a special way.
Hallelujah l-a-lu-ah, I love you Lord today.
Today and tomorrow isn't promised, and only you
deserve this praise.
Hallelujah, hallelujah I give you the highest praise.
Hallelujah, thank you, Lord for loving me in my undone
state,
I'm a miracle in progress and only you know my fate.
I'm saying thank you for providing, protecting, and all
your fatherly ways.
Hallelujah l-a-lu-ah, I love you Lord.
Happy Father's Day

What Does God Think About Sin?

ROMANS 6:23

What Does God Think About Sin?

Riffraff - No good
Trash - Stinks, dirty, full of worms and maggots
A child of God live safe is full of the spirit of God and is not comfortable doing just anything or going anywhere.
But, trash lies where it will or wherever the wind blows.
But, the destiny of trash is in a land field, waiting to be buried, never having a chance of being used again by God or any man.
Once the land is filled, the trash is burnt in an open pit fire, going back to ashes and dust.
Blowing around with no peace, just a tormented soul.
Destination...Hell
The wages of sin is death *(Romans 6:23)*

notes

DATE / /

♥

♥

Why Did You Give Me A Heart So Big?

Why Did You Give Me A Heart So Big?

Why did you give me a heart so big that no one will accept? Why did you give me a heart so big that no one respects the love within?
All I can hear you say is; love, love, and love again.
And even though I'm obedient, all I hear from my broken, scarred and torn heart, that you have mended time and time again from the darts of neglect, disrespect, and abuse is, when will I enjoy the interest that I love so good should reflect?
I say to you, Lord, even in my pain thank you Lord for your unfailing, and un denying love.
You are love and thank you for life.

notes

What Shall I Render Unto Thee?

What Shall I Render Unto Thee?

For what shall I render onto the all I have doesn't
belong to me.
For my Jesus spread His undying love for what none
of us is worthy of.
For all I do in Jesus, sweet name is only to give my
heavenly father the praise.
For I know hallelujah is the highest praise we often
speak.
Yet, the question remains, what shall we render onto
thee?
Yes, fall on bended knees to humble this watch unto
the and give your life to God Almighty, or without him
life could not be.
So, I give all the glory, honor and praise to Jesus and
none to man or me.

To God be the glory, the creative of miracles!!!

Anything Is Possible If We Serve The Lord

ROMANS 5:3-4

Anything Is Possible If We Serve The Lord

Anything is possible, if you serve the Lord, anything, anything, anything. Come me before me in worship with praise and Thanksgiving.

Rejoice in trials, pray, and believe. *(Romans 5:3-4)* Whether it be a fire furnace, whether it be alliance den, or even if you're in prison, Rejoice in praise because anything is possible if you serve the Lord, anything, anything, anything.

He knows every here on your head and they are numbered one by one. *(Luke 12:7)*

If you're in trouble, remember no weapon formed against you shall prosper because he that is in you is greater than he that is in the world. *(Isaiah 54:17 & 1 John 4:4)*
Anything is possible if you serve the Lord, anything, anything, anything.

If you have a need, His word says He shall supply all your needs according to His riches in glory.
(Philippians 4:19)
I own all the land and the cattle on a thousand hills.
(Psalm 50:10-12)

Anything Is Possible If We Serve The Lord

I have never seen the righteous forsaken or His seed begging bread.

Like the lady with the crew of oil and a little flour, or the six thousand fed with two fish and five loaves of bread, trust in the Lord.

Anything is possible if you serve the Lord, anything, anything, anything.

If you need healing, God says humble yourselves before
me and turn from your wicked ways, I shall heal your land.

I am the one who raised Lazarus from the dead, opened Sarah's womb, healed the woman with the issue of blood. And the man with lame of palsy, the little girl who died and her traveled seeking Jesus and the girl was alive and returned. According to your faith, believe and receive.

Anything is possible if you serve the Lord, anything, anything, anything.

Like A Tree

JEREMIAH 17:8

Like A Tree

Denominations are just like a different name of a tree,
but we grow up towards the sun/Son
We are family as long as Jesus is the foundation that
we are planted on.
Jesus is the solid rock in which we stand.
Jesus is the tree of life.
Jesus is the living water in which we thrive
and without Jesus we would not be alive.
Whether we be Baptist, Holiness, Apostolic,
Pentecostal, Methodist, Protestant, Seven Day
Adventist, and the list goes on, but the word of God
says there is no other name in heaven or on earth that
we can be saved by except the name of Jesus.
(Acts 4:12)
There is power in the name of Jesus.
Ttrees have many different names, but it is still a tree.

DATE   /   /

No Reserved Seats

ISAIAH 64:6

No Reserved Seats

Money, tithes and offering can't pay for your seat.
God cannot be bribed, for salvation is free.
Our debt and ransom was paid in full on Calvary!
We are not paying for a style show, for Jesus has
seen us naked, dirty, and in our sin. Jesus is our only
way in.

We can never repay him for all he has done. For all of
our righteousness is of filthy rags, and we are nothing
without Him. *(Isaiah 64:6)*

We are not paying him for a play,
for our old tapes play for free every day.
God's house is not for acting or pretending we were
puppets and zombies.

But, Jesus has all power to set us free.
You don't need money to enter the presence of the
Lord,
just praise and worship.
Our victory is in our praise.

The Lord wants to take us to another place.

People think to live holy is not in style.
just no clothes change, people change, styles
change.

No Reserved Seats

But Jesus is the same today, tomorrow and forever
more. *(Hebrews 13:8)*

So, be a sellout.
For the entrance of the kingdom is sold out.
You cannot enter to the father except through the
son, Jesus. He paid it all.
(John 14:6)

There are no reserve seats.
And yes, tithes and offerings are required of thee.

The Balcony or The Basement

The Balcony or The Basement

The Balcony

Heaven, where you can live life eternally full of peace, love, joy and happiness, praising God all the day long.

The Basement

Hell, a place where there is everlasting torment, screaming, crying and the stench of burning flesh, with
no chance of ever again hearing the voice of God in peace.

The BALCONY of HEAVEN, where God sits high and looks low with eagles eyes.

The BASEMENT, the pit of Hell, Lake of Fire not like most basements. This is not a very cool place. You won't be chillin' there!!

Remember at the concerts no one wanted to sit in the balcony, it was called the nose bleed section?
Some people claimed they couldn't see. Let the truth be known they just wanted to be up close and personal with the entertainer.

The Balcony or The Basement

The balcony just wasn't the "in" thing. So to be in, they would buy a ticket at any price on the ground floor, in the pit, close to the stage. Screaming, clapping, dancing, standing ovations. All kinds of Praise.

In church people run for the balcony to get further away. In the balcony or on the floor, God's people are constantly running for the door while God's message is going forth.

Remember the house parties in the basement? We danced, we sweated, make-up ran, hair fell. We never got too hot, too tired, or too sweaty.

WE HAD IT GOING ON!

In God's house we gotta be cute, can't mess up my suit, not a hair out of place.

While it's time for PRAISE, not many hands are raised.

Praise leaders voices high, congregations voices low, real low, still trying to be entertained.

The Balcony or The Basement

Dance, stand, stomp, waiting to be prompted.

Standing ovation, we need an invitation.

God gave His life!
Where's our sacrifice?
He paid an AWESOME PRICE.
We act nonchalant like...oh well, that was nice.

He's calling us higher.
His desire is that no man should perish, but have everlasting life.

What is the value of your PRAISE?

BALCONY or BASEMENT?
HEAVEN or HELL?

The Divine Storehouse or The Mall

MATTHEW 6:21

The Divine Storehouse or The Mall

I choose the greatest of them all. I shop at Jesus' storehouse where I don't need a dime. It just takes dedication and devotion of your heart, soul and mind. I know a lot of people give their all at the malls, but for what cause? It puts them in debt and depression, worry sets in then collection agencies call to collect and they have no respect. For all they want is your paycheck.

You do have a choice to serve Jesus or man, Jesus has the divine plan. I shop with Jesus at the divine storehouse where there are no payments, no credit checks and I receive utmost respect. There is NO charge, for Jesus paid the ultimate price payment long ago. All you have t o do i s follow the straight and narrow road that in the end is paved with pure gold.

Everything you receive will be a blessing and they are free. Come as you are and He will remove every flaw. He will save you money and, more importantly, your soul from hell where all vain, ungodly people are going to go.
(Matthew 6:21)

The Divine Storehouse or The Mall

Give the goods to Jesus' storehouse where you won't be cheated or robbed. "For where your treasure is, there will your heart be also." You won't need a safe, for Jesus is the safest place, for He is a strong tower, you won't need a cedar chest or moth balls for it i s written, "Lay not up for yourselves treasures upon the earth, where moth and rust doth corrupt, and where thieves break through and steal: but lay up for yourselves treasures i n heaven, where neither moth nor rust doth corrupt, and where thieves do not break through nor steal." *(Matthew 6:19-24)*

The policy at the storehouse is "Ask and it shall be given you; seek, and ye shall find; knock, and it shall be opened unto you. For everyone that asketh, receiveth; and he that seeketh, findeth; and to him that knocketh, it shall be opened." *(Matthew 7:7-8)*

So fellowship together in worship and praise because walking with Jesus pays.

To God be all the glory, the creator of miracles!

DATE / /

♥

I'm A Child of The King

HEBREWS 13:5

I'm A Child of The King

I am a child of the King and I have been redeemed.
I have no regrets and I deserve respect.
My father has a plan and I will trust m y lite in His
hands.

He said He will never leave or forsake me and I will go
wherever He takes me. *(Hebrews 13:5)*
There's no mountain too high or valley too low that my
God doesn't know.

So wherever life takes me,
I know that my Jesus will save me.
l am the head and not the tail and I trust in Jesus, He
cannot fail. *(Deuteronomy 28:13)*

I Will Praise You Lord Because You Reign

PSALM 34:1

I Will Praise You Lord Because You Reign

I will praise you Lord because you reign.
I will praise you when I'm blue and my heart's filled
with gloom.
I will praise you Lord when my life is full of drought
and famine.
I will praise you Lord through the storm and all turmoil.
I will praise you Lord in my achievements and all my
success.
I will praise you Lord when life is at a stand still and I'm
usually stressed.
will praise you Lord because l am blessed.

I will praise you Lord for all you've done.
I praise you Lord and give thanks for your Son
I praise you Lord because you are the author and
finisher of my faith.
I praise you Lord because only with you can I win this
Christian race.
So, I say thank you Jesus for your blood and thank you
Father for all your love.

I give you the highest praise hallelujah and amen for
no one else deserves this praise throughout the land.
I praise you Lord and can't say thank you enough, but
thanks for bringing me out of all my stuff.

I Will Praise You Lord Because You Reign

When praises go up,
Blessings come down.
Thank you Lord for
Turning my life around.

"Your praises shall continually be in my mouth at all times."
(Psalm 34:1 & Philippians 4:18)

Thank God I Can Feel

Thank God I Can Feel

Sometimes I feel alone or even depressed, and I take a look around and realized I'm blessed.
Sometimes I feel good, sometimes I feel bad, but I thank God I can feel because I could be dead.
Sometimes I feel full of energy and ready to run a race and I slowed down to thank God for His amazing grace. Sometimes I feel guilty because I have sinned or stepped out of God's will again, and I thank God for having mercy on my soul and forgiving me over and over again.
Sometimes I feel tired and I just wanna sleep and I thank God for forgiving me perfect peace.
Sometimes I feel indecisive and don't know what to do and I thank God for a sound mind and choices too.
All the time I have desires of a human and want the company of a companion.
And all the time I bow down and thank God for my salvation and making me who I am.

To God be the glory the creator of miracles!!

notes
DATE   /   /

I Will Praise God & Give Thanks For Another Day

PSALM 118:24

I Will Praise God & Give Thanks For Another Day

Whether the sun shines,
Or if it rains.
Whether the sky is blue,
Or if it's gray.
Whether there is a drought,
Or if there is a flood.
Whether there is peace,
Or storms through the land.
I will praise God
And give thanks for another day!
For this is the day that the Lord has made,
And I will rejoice
And be glad in it. *(Psalm 118:24)*

DATE   /   /

Remember Always, You Are Not Alone

ROMANS 12:1

Remember Always, You Are Not Alone

Remember you are never alone for Jesus has a home. He lives and dwells deep within a temple that we call our body, yet it is not our own. Where ever you go you are never alone. The loneliness that we feel is only one of the devils many schemes to make us feel like giving up when we've already won. All we have to do is reach for our Heavenly Fathers hand.

Loneliness is when your hearts filled with pain and you feel like your going insane. Loneliness is when the devil fills your mind with lies and deceit and causes this sinful flesh to become weak. When flesh becomes weak you seek a soft warm body that only satisfies you for a moment and leaves. When it's flesh that you seek, you only become more weak because it is full of sin and soon all sin is going to come to terrible end.

When trouble never seems to end, darkness and fear comes to haunt you again and again. When a voice keeps saying your no good, your a failure and you just want to die. Well when you go to your secret place and cry and your screaming voice says "Oh My God Why!!!" Just remember satan is a liar and he's destined to eternal fire.

Remember Always, You Are Not Alone

Like everyone on this earth, he has a job to do and his job is to steal, kill, and destroy. He does it by causing confusion, fear, illusions, manipulation; whatever it takes to destroy a soul. Because as we know, misery loves company and when your
miserable you don't love anything not even yourself. Our job is to commit our bodies and lives as a living sacrifice *(Romans 12:1)* to Christ to be as an example to others. It may seem that we've been lost down stream, yet deep inside you hear a faint voice scream, "Its Going To Be Alright You've Got To Fight."

You are not alone for the battles already won. Hold to your Heavenly Fathers hand for only He has the master plan.

This flesh is weak so continue to pray and seek the God Almighty of your belief. You are not alone and will soon be home with our true friend whom you can depend. He won't leave you holding the bag, for He picks up all slack.

He has many names yet he is the one who can do all things. Just trust and believe. You are truly free. You will not be deceived. Seek his face even in that place. He will give you grace.

Remember Always, You Are Not Alone

For his grace is sufficient for thee and in Him you should believe. For He gave up His life on Calvary. When he died and went to hell, he paid for all of our sins so that we wouldn't ever have to see what real the torture of hell.

When He rose again, He had the keys with him. Giving all power unto Him so that we may have peace, love, joy, contentment, long suffering. All of the fruits of the spirit, if we humble our ourselves unto Him. Love Him with all your heart, mind, and soul, and He and only He can make us whole.

He can fill the empty space in the pit of your stomach that earthly food can't fill. Even the special fleshly person in your life can't fill. Not even all the money or the most potent drug in the world can't take away. He can even mend a broken heart. No matter what the situation seems to be just take a closer walk with thee. Where He is the way the truth and the life and there's no darkness with Him or in Him.

Just remember, you are never alone. He's calling you. Won't you come back home?

God be the glory the creator of miracles!!!

notes

God Is Good

God Is Good

God is good, God is great,
I am thankful that He sealed my fate.
My fate is abundant life instead of a sinful death,
Instead God gave me His ruach breath.
I am promised eternal life because I gave my life to
Christ,
It is the best decision I ever made because God is
good and He sealed my fate.
His grace and mercy brought me through,
He gave me a life brand new.
God's joy gives me strength to endure life day to day,
His peace helps me to stand through whatever life
brings my way.
God is good, God is great,
I am thankful that He sealed my fate.
He loves me more than I can ever explain,
He collects my tears and He heals my pain.
I'm a pilgrim passing through,
This world is not my home but while I'm here I will be
sure to share my testimony and all that God can do.
God is good, God is great,
I am thankful that He sealed my fate.
My life is no longer filled with stress and strife,
My name is written in the lambs book of life.
God's love is pure and true,
He will never leave or forsake you.

God Is Good

He's not like man who can lie,
God provides, He protects.
He cared so much that He wrapped Himself in flesh.
And came to earth as a baby growing into a man,
To walk the earth to see what we experience and
never did He sin.
He experienced all sorts of hatred, deceit, temptation,
demons and sin.
He was sin free.
He remained focused living on purpose fulfilling the
Father's plan.
Holy and righteous,
He took the beating He did not deserve.
While being tortured and close to death, He still had
us on His mind.
He said "Father forgive them for they know not what
they do," and hung His head and died.
He went to hell and rose again with all power in His
hands.
Even then before He left He said "I go to prepare a
place for you. In my father's house are many mansions
and if it was not so I would not tell you."
And He promised to send back a comforter which is
the Holy Spirit which gives us power and lives and
dwells in us.
God is good, God is great,
I am thankful that He sealed my fate.

Because Jesus Loves Me

Because Jesus Loves Me

I don't care what you think of me.
I don't care if you like me.
Because Jesus loves me.
I don't care who you call me.
I don't care if you talk about me.
Because Jesus loves me.
I don't care if you support me.
I don't care if you see me cry.
Because Jesus love me.
I don't care if you like my praise.
I don't care if you think that I'm insane.
Because Jesus loves me.
I don't care if you like my dance.
I don't care if you like how I clap my hands.
Because Jesus loves me.
All I'm saying is that I'm only trying to please Jesus,
not man because only Him I can depend.
He paid an awesome price for me so that I could be
free.
When Jesus (God) created me he said that I am good,
very good.
He calls me righteous and holy.
Jesus had mercy on me and loved me through my
mess.

Because Jesus Loves Me

He encouraged me to go through every trial and test.
Jesus, save me by His grace and said "you can win
this race." You shall live and not die, I am here by your
side."
"Hold onto me, my daughter and I will hold onto you."
" I will never leave you, I will see you through."
He said, I am victorious and more than a conqueror.
So, I don't care what you say, think or do.
I'm here to please Jesus not you.
I'm going to praise him while I can.
 Because He is my everything and all that I am.
He is my father, my mother, my brother, my friend.
He is my comforter, provider, protector.
He is the lover of my soul and my savior.
He never gets tired, to him I can always go.
I don't care what you say, do or where you go. I love
you.
I'm only responsible for my soul.

DATE   /   /

♥

Knock & The Door Shall Be Opened

MATTHEW 7:7-8

Knock & The Door Shall Be Opened

Hello my friend, I'm right here to give you a hand. I've come to let you know that you don't have to go down that dark and dreary road, for you are being used to commit your own murder.

I am knocking won't you let me in for I am your only true friend. I've come to let you know that you don't have to go down that dreadful road. I've carried your cross., suffered, bled, died, laid in a borrowed tomb, and rose again with all power in my hands. *(1 Corinthians 15:4)* Power over death, hell and the grave *(Revelation 1:18)*

I am the Lord! I have joy that you won't find in drugs, so won't you give me a chance to show my love? I have the creator of heaven and earth. I even knew you before your birth. *(Jeremiah 1:5)* No matter what sin that has you bound I have the power to put your feet on solid ground.

Remember you have a friend and I'm here to give you a hand. *(John 15:13)* the battles of this life. You will never win unless you let me in. *(Deuteronomy 20:4 & Exodus 14:14)* I will never enter about force with a choice is yours. Yet I am watching the score.

Knock & The Door Shall Be Opened

You know that you are losing and stay ahead., if you let him have the victory, your end is death.

Once again, I have come to give you a hand won't you let me in? It's never too late as long as you have a life you can defeat the angel of death. Just call on my name Jesus Christ for I am waiting to give you new life.

Don't worry just relax and army of angels have already been dispatched. No need to place blame or even be ashamed. *(Romans 8:1)* just make high ground your aim. Press toward the mark of the high calling of Jesus Jesus Christ. *(Philippians 3:14)*

You don't have to die in the way sin has made your life, but I have power to deliver you out every vice. *(John 8:36)* I will never leave or forsake you, *(Deuteronomy 31:8)* that you can always trust in lean on and depend. So open the door, I am knocking grab a hold of my unchanging hand.

There is hope for tomorrow won't you let me take away your sorrow.

notes

DATE   /   /

He Will Take Control

GALATIANS 5:16

He Will Take Control

I know that I am not in control,
For only Jesus, blood has made me whole.
Jesus died as a living sacrifice.
For our Heavenly Father, we must surrender our life.
For the Holy Ghost can rid you of every vice.
For without Jesus, you have no life.
He will give you joy divine.
He will even give you peace of mind.
He will keep you when your flesh doesn't want to be kept.
Keep your mind on Jesus.
Stop, pray, listen, look ahead,
Follow the Holy Spirit *(Galatians 5:16, 22-24)*
Take one step, don't worry I think about the rest.
Have faith, trust in Jesus.
The Holy Spirit knows was best.
Jesus is the way, the truth and the life.
The Holy Spirit will guide you into all truth. *(John 16:13)*
Hold to Jesus hold hands.
For He and only He has control over this land and every man.
Jesus holds the master plan.
 God said " for know the plans that I have for you,
 plans to prosper you and not to harm you to give you hope and a future." *(Jeremiah 29:11)*

I Am A Woman

PSALM 139:14

I Am A Woman

I am a woman
I was created from the rib of a man
I walked beside him, I hold his hand
I support him, not push him
I pray him through his fears
I plan to be with him throughout all his years
I am a woman
I am feminine, yet, I am strong
I don't put myself in a man's place
Because I would be wrong
God created the woman for the man
And until he comes, I will stand
God is with me, I have no fears
For God, comforts me and collects all of my tears
When I am weak, God is strong
He is a keeper through any storm
He created me to endure
With him fighting battles I have won many wars
I am victorious
I am a queen
I am a woman
Fearfully and wonderfully made in the image of God
(Psalm 139:14)
I reign supreme

notes

DATE   /   /

♥

Life Is A Test

EPHESISNS 6:13

Life Is A Test

You are tested every minute of every day.
You will be tested all the way.
Will you stand, will you fall?
When you're backs against the wall
and it seems there's nothing you can do, nothing at all.
Whether you stand or if you fall,
On Jesus name you can call.
Tests has been here since the beginning of time,
just make sure that you have a made up mind.
When your patients have been worn thin
and when you're at your wits end,
and it seems that people keep stepping on your toes.
Remember Jesus knows.
It's spiritual warfare that we're in.
Our fight is not against flesh and blood, but against
spirits and principalities and high places.
Will you stand or will you fall?
Jesus says stand *(Ephesians 6:13)* and not faint.
(Galatians 6:9)
So stand, stand tall.
Looking towards the hills for where cometh your help.
(Psalm 121:1–2)
For Jesus is a very present help and the time of
trouble *(Psalm 46:1)*

Life Is A Test

If you fall, fall on bended knees, and pray.
Get back up giving God the praise with victory in Jesus.
Remember, joy cometh in the morning. *(Psalm 30:5)*
The battle is already won.
Jesus is a very present help in the time of trouble. *(Psalm 46:1)*

notes

Jesus Loves Us All

EVERYBODY NEEDS LOVE

MATTHEW 22:39

Jesus Loves Us All

Jesus loves all of His children.
He created us all.
Whether we are black, blue, purple, yellow, green, red or white, every soul is precious in His sight.
He commands us to love our neighbor as ourselves. *(Matthew 22:39)*
Whether they be gay, straight, lesbian, heterosexual, homosexual or trans.
Male, female, child, man, woman, boy or girl, young or old,
Jesus loves us all and we should love everybody.
Jesus commands us to love one another as He has loved us. *(John 13:34)*
Love our neighbor as thyself. *(Matthew 22:39)*
Jesus is our judge. It is our duty to love. *(1 Peter 4:8)*
"Above all love each other deeply because love covers and multitude of sins."
(Proverbs 10:12) hatred, throws up strife, but love covers all sin.
Remember none of us are perfect. *(Romans 3:23)*
For I'll have sand and fallen short of the glory of God.
Everybody needs love and Jesus loves us all. *(John 15:12–13)*
 God, so loved the world that he gave his only begotten son that whomever believes in him, should not perish be happy eternal life. *(John 3:16)*

I Am Not A Saint

CORINTHIANS 15:31

I'm Not A Saint

I'm not claiming to be a saint because that, I ain't.
I am a child of God, on Him I depend.
I have learned to hold onto His unchanging hands.
I'm reaching for the prize,
That I will receive in heaven's blue skies.
Saints are home with the Lord,
Where He is worshipped and adored.
But no, I have not arrived.
I'm on the ground floor.
I have not yet finished my course.
Yes I have been saved by His amazing grace.
I have been sanctified, set apart, connected to His heart.
A peculiar people.
I have been delivered from the enemies hand.
Yet, I still live with sin.
I have to kill my flesh again and again.
(Corinthians 15:31)
Repent, die out to the old man.
I am a new creation. All things pass away, and all things become new. *(2 Corinthians 5:17)*
On Jesus, the solid rock I stand. All of the ground is sinking sand.
I've searched my soul, I've purged my heart.
I'm off to a winning start.
 I fell down and gotten back up. *(Ecclesiastes 9:11)*

I'm Not A Saint

"The race is not given to the swift, nor the battle to the strong, but the one that endures to the end shall be saved." *(Matthew 24:13)*
When I have entered heavens gate, where Jesus welcomes me with my white robe and my crown adorned with gems,
On judgment day when I hear " well done, good and faithful servant. Thou has been faithful over a few things, I will make you ruler over many. Enter thou into the joy of the Lord." *(Matthew 25:23)*
Then I will be a saint.

notes

DATE   /   /

With God I Beat All The Odds

ACTS 2:38

With God I Beat All The Odds

Three generations of the divorce included mine; grandparents, parents and myself.
Three generations of infidelity, sexual abuse, rape (childhood and adult), domestic violence.
Three generations of failed relationships, rejection, promiscuity and shattered dreams.
Three generations of heartbreak and pain, drug addiction in alcoholism.

Life without Jesus is full of these things. It happens in cycles and generations over and over again. Until you accept Jesus Christ in your life, it will never end. It feels like a roller coaster, ferris wheel and merry-go-round all in one. Satan is the conductor and it's no fun. Playing Russian roulette with a fully loaded gun. I don't have a sad story or a woe it's me. I give God all the glory. I accepted the invitation to accept Christ in my life; to repent and be baptized and I did receive the Holy Spirit. *(Acts2:38)* The free gift of salvation *(Ephesians 2:8–9)*

Jesus, didn't have to do it but He did. He gave up His life for me to live. I could have died as a child in the middle of violence, abuse, and rape. I beat the odds that's what statistics say.

With God I Beat All The Odds

I could have contracted Aids or OD'd. I was in the midst of danger and many times I escaped. I could have been a Jane Doe on a hot summer day in the alley. But because I called on Jesus, He caused my enemy to help me up and his helpers to flee the other way.

I thank God for the people in my life that took me to church. They taught me how to pray, gave me a Bible and even provided a safe place to stay. God has been good to me. He has kept me along the way.

notes
DATE   /   /

I Stand On The Promises Of God

PSALM 46:1

I Stand On The Promises Of God

I stand on His promises and give Him all the praise. Thank you, God, the father for coming down from your throne in glory to save the day. The father God, being a spirit wrapped himself in flesh born of a virgin. His name, Jesus.

Jesus was born to show the way to live, to walk, to talk, to speak and believe. Jesus walked the Earth to experience all of our pain. On Calvary cross, He shed His blood to pay a debt we couldn't even repay. For the wages of our sins was more than all the money in the land. Jesus was the only one created worthy to fulfill the plan.

Today, Lord, I just want to say thank you as I bow down humbly to say I love you. I live today because God is powerful. He is mighty. His word is true. I have victory in Jesus. My name is written in the lambs book of life. It has been signed. I have been sealed. I am delivered and set free a living testimony. Jesus paid it all for you and for me.

Scriptures to stand on:
"God is my refuge and my strength a very present help in the time of trouble." *(Psalm 46:1)*
"God is my deliverer. He delivers me out of the hands of the enemy." *(Psalm 59:1)*

Jesus I Can't Thank You Enough

I'M TRULY GRATEFUL

ROMANS 8:34

Jesus I Can't Thank You Enough

Thank you Jesus.
Thank you Lord for the awesome price that you paid.
Laying down Your life was the ultimate sacrifice.
Thank you for the marvelous gifts of life.
Not just life, but life more abundant.
Thank you for Your love that overcomes every
disappointment.
Thank you for salvation,
the gift that you give so freely.
Thank you Jesus for Your blood shed.
You did what no one else could do.
Your blood shed on Calvary for me and all humanity.
We were bound in sin.
Your blood paid sins ransom and set the captives
free.
No longer bound by the weight of sin.
You turned my life around.
This is not where the story ends.
You didn't stay down.
You died but rose again.
Jesus you live.
You sit at the right hand of the Father interceding on
our behalf *(Romans 8:34)*
But you sent back a friend, the comforter.
Holy Spirit that keeps me.

Jesus I Can't Thank You Enough

Thank you Jesus for the angels that you dispatched to watch over and protect me and minister to all my needs *(Psalm 91:11–12)*
Thank you Jesus for being a promise keeper.
Leading me out of the depths of hell,
for your word directs my path.
Thank you, thank you, thank you Jesus,
for saving, loving, caring and seeing about me.
Thank you Jesus for providing every need.
For being faithful, trustworthy, answering prayer,
protecting and being everything to me.
Thank you Jesus for taking care of me and trusting and believing in me.
There is nothing greater.
Nothing can or ever will be all that You are and have been to me.
Jesus, You gave the best present, the best gift that can ever be.
Nothing from a man, woman, boy, girl, or family.
Nothing under the tree can ever stop what you have done for me.
Thank you Jesus for everything that You are to me.

I Put My Trust In Jesus

PSALM 50:10

I Put My Trust In Jesus

On Jesus the solid rock I stand,
I keep my eyes on the prize.
Jesus is a mighty fortress,
In Him I will abide.
Trusting Him to be my guide.
Before I knew Jesus, I trusted man.
I was lost, but Jesus paid the awesome cost.
I was lost, but now I am found.
I'm no longer on shaky ground.
Jesus loves me and that's no lie.
On Calvary He bled, died and rose again so that I
could have a life.
I love Jesus because He first loved me.
He loved me when my life was out of control.
He took me in to have to hold,
To remake and mold.
I was broken and He made me whole.
I was wounded and scared.
Jesus was always there.
Without Him, I could never have survived.
With His love and grace, I thrived.
No one else can I always trust, lean on and depend.
Nobody but my father who owns the cattle on a
thousand hills *(Psalm 50:10)* all the houses and all of
the land. *(Psalm 24:1)*
My Father will supply every need. *(Philippians 4:19)*
I am a child of the Almighty King.

notes

DATE / /

♥

Everyday Is Thanksgiving

PSALM 136:1

Everyday Is Thanksgiving

Today and everyday, I can say Happy Thanksgiving.
"Oh give thanks unto the Lord for He is good."
(Psalm 136:1)
I am happy because this is another day that God woke me
up and allowed me to see His beautiful portraits in the sky.
To see the trees, the grass, all the different people, animals
and all of creation.
To live, move, and have my being. *(Acts 17:28)* I am
thankful because God sent His only son for me.
(John 3:16)
Jesus willingly laid down His life for you and me. God's
desire is that no man should perish, but that we have
everlasting in eternal life.
 Thanksgiving is not about pilgrims on the Mayflower or the
feast. It is about our relationship with God. All that He has
done and all that He is still doing and yet to do.
We are the pilgrims passing through. *(1 Peter 2:11)* We are
aliens and strangers of this land. *(1 Peter 2:9-12)* Heaven
is our home as saints. Because of this, I don't let things of
this world, discouraged me.
Jesus covers me, I am safe. I praise God, my savior and
creative with Thanksgiving because of who He is and all He
has done for me. I am thankful that Jesus shared His blood
for me on calvary. His blood covers my sins and all of my
dirty deeds. My heart was filled with filth, lust, greed, lies,
and deceit, but Jesus.

Everyday Is Thanksgiving

I am grateful that Jesus took the beating that we all deserve, but could never withstand. He didn't just bleed and die. He rose again with the keys, taking power over death, hell and the grave. *(Revelation 1:18)* Jesus showed grace and mercy. He did not let me die.
Jesus came that we have life in life more abundantly. Satan, our enemy comes to steal, kill and destroy.
(John 10:10) Just still out of joy, our strength, kill our purpose, vision destroy our family and our future. His planned failed. Satan is defeated. There is victory in Jesus. Jesus love through the word of God, washed away all shame and guilt, now I am free.
I am here today to share His word that if you are lost that you may be found. I lift up the mighty and powerful name of Jesus. I am happy. I am thankful. I give God praise with a cheerful heart.

Happy Thanksgiving

DATE   /   /

Sammie

Sammie

I had an offer to meet a dog and possibly take him home.
I thought about it, and thought about it, I had to ask the rest of the family.
I went to meet this puppy dog.
I seen him, and he seen me.
He ran from me.
I ask why they wanted to get rid of him. The answer was that he barked too much and the neighbors complained.
I gave him a ride in my truck and took him in to meet the family.
He was so nervous.
I could tell that he had been hurt, even abused, but he didn't even speak.
He didn't growl, or bark. He never complained. He just ran, ducked, or hid.
I loved him.
He had no training, he couldn't climb stairs, he had no home training, and he wasn't even house broken.
I loved him.
He didn't know common commands, he didn't have a tickle spot, he didn't even kiss or like his belly rubbed, he didn't even respond to love. He didn't know how to love.
I made the call and the final decision the he was going to be a part of the family.
The first thing that we did is change his name to Sammie.
He had a name, two bags of food, and one toy.
I loved him, trained him, nurtured him, and mothered him.

Sammie

He ran and hid just for a little while.

I continued to love him, chase him and clean up after him and protect him.

He was a blessing to me. The name h e came with was from another planet, Cosmo. When I looked at him being so small, his eye shape, and the amount of energy he had I thought of Sammy Davis Jr. tap dancing or Sammie Sosa the baseball player.

Well he was family my Sammie. Before it was over, he knew it all.

He was my love, my baby.

I seen something in Sammie I never seen before in an animal, it was as if he were a little man in a little puppies body.

I adopted him.

He was so timid, so small, so fragile, so frail, just an empty shell, he just existed and needed someone to spend time with him and love him.

I loved him, I didn't know why.

He even looked like a rat at times.

I loved him, I saw potential.

He was a Jack Russell Terrier. He was so cute, so full of energy, he ran jumped, leaped, barked, played, followed commands, and h e even learned how to beg.

My Sammie gave me kisses.

Sammie

He loved me, he greeted me, he snuggled with me, he never was far away, and when I was sick he was there, he sleep under the bed.

I love him, he loved me.

Sammie loved everybody.

He was so loveable, huggable, cute, strong, and energetic.

I loved him.

He was so loyal, so sweet.

Sammie's time with me was short.

He had to go home.

I prayed, I nursed him, I took him to the veterinarian, yes I spent money on him and I loved him. I would do anything for my Sammie.

I did everything I could do. We came together as a family and worked together to try to keep him here with us, just get him well, but God's Will Be Done.

Sammie wasn't just a puppy or a dog, he was an angel in disguise, and he was a lesson on how short our time together could be.

He was a lesson on true love, second chances, and family.

Sammie was a fighter until the end, until he laid his head down and put on that cheesy grin showing those pretty teeth.

He was a handsome little man. I will always remember Sammie he left me with some beautiful memories.

He was a loyal friend. I wish I could have given him a proper burial, a home going service, he deserved the best.

Sammie

I won't say that I lost anything because he left m e a lot, but I will say I miss him and if men are dogs I would have Sammie.

Dedicated to my Sammie
You're the best
Love Always

Oh What A Glorious Day It Will Be When I See The King

Oh What A Glorious Day It Will Be When I See The King

No one understands God's great master plan and one day this life on earth he's to end.

I ran this race at an awesome pace, some days up and some days down, some for many years around and around. Oh what a glorious day it will be when I go home to see the King.

The race is not given to the strong or the swift, but to the one that endureth to the end.

I've finished my course and been a witness for the Lord. So say goodbye, don't you cry, for this is a glorious day. No more heartache, no more pain.

Oh what a glorious day it will be when I go home to see the King. Oh what a celebration, it shall be praising and rejoicing. I am free.

This is a day to remember; singing praises, flowers, limos, and traffic stopped for me with a long precession of friends and family.

Oh what a glorious day it will be when I go home to see the King.

Oh What A Glorious Day It Will Be When I See The King

Everyone takes time out to say their last good-byes, focusing just on me.

Oh what a glorious day it will be when I go to see the King. Some will cry and not understand why, but death is the way of eternal rest and there I have been freed.

So sing and rejoice with the angels, remembering all the good times and oh what a glorious day it will bring.

I am with the King.

notes

DATE   /   /

What Is A Veteran?

What Is A Veteran?

VETERAN

```
a   n       r   x   e   u       e
l   d       a   u   s   d       i
i   u       i   b   o   a       g
a   r       n   e   l   c       h
n   a       e   r   u   i       b
t   n       d   a   t   o       o
    c           n   e   u       r
    e           t       s
```

notes

DATE   /   /

♥

Chase God, He Is Your Answer

REVELATIONS 1:8

Chase God, He Is Your Answer

Glory be to God on high.

The miracle work, our creator.

The giver of life, our savior.

Healer and deliverer.

"The Alpha and Omega.

The beginning and the end."

(Revelations 1:8, 17–18, 21:6 & 22:13)

The author and finisher of our faith. *(Hebrews 12:2)*

He is the one that created the heavens and the earth.

(Genesis 1:1)

The sun, moon, stars and the sky.

You may feel like giving up, or feel like a failure and like your life is spiraling out of control,

Surrender to God.

Remember that you cannot win in your own strength.

The word of God says "the battle is not our own, it is the Lord's." *(2 Chronicles 20:15)*

"The battle is not won by power nor by might, but by the spirit of the Lord." *(Zechariah 4:6)*

Take a deep breath.

Praise God that you are still alive.

"Cast all your cares upon Him for He cares for you."

(1 Peter 5:7)

Jesus says "come to me all that are weary and burdened and I will give you rest."

Chase God, He Is Your Answer

"Take my yoke upon you and learn of me, but I am gentle and humble in heart, and I will find rest for your souls. From my yoke is easy and my burden is light."
(Matthew 11:28–30)

"Greater is He that is in you than He that is in the world."
(1 John 4:4)

God is with you.

Speak life, make a declaration to yourself.

I shall live and not die!

There is power in what you say to yourself, about yourself, your situations and others. *(Proverbs 18:24)*

You may feel defeated but when you put your trust in Jesus you shall come out victorious.

Know that you can do all things through Christ Jesus who strengthens you. *(Philippians 4:13)*

"We are more than conquerors through Christ Jesus who strengthens us." *(Romans 8: 37)*

"I will lift my eyes into the hills from whence cometh my help. My help cometh from the Lord, which made heaven and earth." *(Psalm 121:1-2)*

"If God be for us who can be against us?" *(Romans 8:31)*

The answer is nobody. "No weapon formed against thee shall prosper." *(Isaiah 54:17)*

"For we rest not against flash and blood, but against spiritual wickedness and principalities in high places."
(Ephesians 6:12)

Chase God, He Is Your Answer

"For though we walk in flesh we do not war after the flesh."
"The weapons of our warfare are not carnal, but mighty
through God." *(2 Corinthians 10:3–4)*
No matter what may come your way; heartbreak,
relationship, problems, debt, betrayal, addiction, abuse,
neglect, loss of a loved one, etc. You can stand and
knowing God said He'll never leave you nor forsake you.
(Isaiah 41:10, Joshua 1:5 & Deuteronomy 31:8)
Know God said " my grace is sufficient for thee. For my
strength is made perfect and weakness." For when I am
weak, I am strong. *(2 Corinthians 12:9–10)*
When you feel trapped call on God.
God is our refuge and strength a very present help in the
time of trouble. *(Psalm 46:1)*
Make a conscious decision to proclaim God's promise over
your life. Live life and live more abundant. *(John 10:10)*
It's not too late. You're not too far gone.
Jesus knows all about all of your dirty deeds called sin.
He knew that we could not save ourselves that's why He
took the beating.
He carried the cross.
He had nails and his hands and feet.
He wore the crown of thorns, had a sword in His side, spit
on, talked about, and mocked.
But He stayed on the cross, hung His head bled and died.

Chase God, He Is Your Answer

In three days, He rose again with all power in His hands. He did what no one else could do for the remission of our sins.

Reflection Scriptures:
(Matthew 27, Mark 15, Luke 23, John 19, Isaiah 53, 1 Corinthians 15:3, Colossians 2:14)
He is a forgiving God and nothing is too hard for him. **(Jeremiah 32:17)**

"Seek the Lord while he may be found." **(Isaiah 56:6)**

About The Author

Barbara Simpson Saxon was born and raised in Delaware, Ohio, during a time when the city still carried a small-town, country feel. Her early years were shaped by resilience, family roots, and faith, including a close and formative bond with her maternal grandparents, Rachael and George C. Blake.

After her mother found the courage to leave an abusive marriage, Barbara relocated to Columbus, Ohio, where she learned early on the value of perseverance, responsibility, and strength. From the age of ten, she worked diligently to help ease the burdens placed on her family, developing a deep sense of discipline and purpose that would carry her through life.

About The Author

Barbara graduated from Linden McKinley High School and later attended college in 1980. As a young wife and mother, her educational journey was interrupted by domestic violence and the eventual dissolution of her marriage. Despite these challenges, she pressed forward, raising her children and overcoming profound struggles including abuse, addiction, mental health battles, deception, and loss.

Through every trial, Barbara discovered that placing God above all else was the key to survival, healing, and transformation. Her life stands as a testament to God's saving grace, mercy, and unfailing love. A survivor in every sense of the word, Barbara writes from lived experience, offering words of encouragement, faith, and hope to those navigating their own storms.

Through her poetry, Barbara shares not only her journey, but God's promises reminding readers that no matter how broken the past may be, purpose, redemption, and new life are always possible through Christ.